CHINA'S RISE
—— AND THE ——
NEW AGE OF GOLD

How Investors Can Profit
from a Changing World

STEPHEN LEEB, PhD

and

DONNA LEEB

New York   Chicago   San Francisco   Athens   London
Madrid   Mexico City   Milan   New Delhi
Singapore   Sydney   Toronto

1 2 3 4 5 6 7 8 9   LCR   25 24 23 22 21 20

ISBN   978-1-260-44127-7
MHID   1-260-44127-X

e-ISBN   978-1-260-44128-4
e-MHID   1-260-44128-8

This publication is designed to provide accurate and authoritative information in regard to the subject matter covered. It is sold with the understanding that neither the author nor the publisher is engaged in rendering legal, accounting, securities trading, or other professional services. If legal advice or other expert assistance is required, the services of a competent professional person should be sought.

—From a Declaration of Principles Jointly Adopted
by a Committee of the American Bar Association
and a Committee of Publishers and Associations

McGraw Hill books are available at special quantity discounts to use as premiums and sales promotions or for use in corporate training programs. To contact a representative, please visit the Contact Us pages at www.mhprofessional.com.

Contents

Preface

IN LATE 2019, I sent what I believed would be my final draft of *China's Rise and the New Age of Gold* to my editors at McGraw Hill. The book predicted that within coming decades, the world would experience a massive bull market in gold. What did I mean by *massive*? How about gold reaching $20,000 an ounce or higher?

I expected two developments to underpin this enormous rise. Both were pegged to the rise of China and, more generally, of the East. One was that China's continued heavy investment in infrastructure in the developing world would lead to commodity scarcities and rising commodity prices, conditions that historically have gone hand in hand with bull markets in gold. Even more significant, I believed that China would successfully create a new gold-backed monetary reserve system that in the East and eventually likely beyond would largely supersede the dollar.

I noted that China's rising global clout, which made these plans achievable, hadn't happened in a vacuum. It was enabled by a long-term decline in American life that started as far back as the early 1970s—coinciding, not so coincidentally, with the United States' abandonment of the postwar Bretton Woods arrangement that had pegged the dollar to gold. The decline was marked by faltering productivity, a debilitating rise in economic inequality, and the ascendance of a bloated and nonproductive financial sector. I argued that the best hope for the United States was to cooperate as broadly as possible with

China in mutually productive ways rather than to view the world as a zero-sum arena in which China has become our chief foe.

I believed that I had presented a compelling case, identifying a constellation of trends and events that pointed to an unprecedented rise in gold. I still do.

But not long after I turned in the book, COVID-19 made its unwelcome appearance in the world, wreaking havoc and tragedy on a global scale. As 2020 has progressed, the coronavirus has changed life as we know it in ways that months earlier would have been unimaginable. Beyond the impact on daily life and the horror of so many lives lost, it has slammed economic activity, caused financial markets to plummet before starting to recover, sent oil prices skidding, and much more.

There was no way I could simply ignore the pandemic or fail to think long and hard about how it might bear on the geopolitical trends I had seen as leading inexorably to far higher gold prices. What will it mean for China's place in the world? For America's place in the world? For the outlook for global growth? And, my end point, what will it mean for the outlook for gold?

These weren't questions I could even attempt to tackle in the virus's first days, when almost nothing about it was clear. A lot still remains unknown, of course. But now, a few months further along, the smoke has cleared enough that I can start to make some reasoned assessments. And so far it appears that, if anything, the pandemic will only accelerate the shift in power and influence from West to East that is at the heart of the case for a forthcoming huge bull market in gold.

The first question I had to answer was how the pandemic has affected China's economic and geopolitical standing. Clearly, in the early stages of the virus outbreak in Wuhan, China tried to suppress and downplay news of the outbreak, and I have no doubt that it has understated its number of cases and deaths. Still, and whether or not you think its tactics were unnecessarily harsh, China appears to have successfully brought the outbreak under control.

As of now, China is opening up its economy, which seems on track to reverse the steep contraction—of 6 percent—in 2020's first quarter and to resume a respectable level of growth. China has reported positive economic numbers from factory surveys, and electricity consumption has been rising, pieces of hard data that indicate a relatively fast recovery.

More generally, the East has fared better with COVID-19 than has the West. To give one remarkable statistic, as of early May, the total number of COVID-19 deaths just in New York State—with a population of around 19.4 million—tops reported deaths from the virus from the entire rest of the world.

There could be any number of explanations, from the East's greater prior experience dealing with viruses, to better-managed healthcare systems, to cultural norms, to the possibility that the West may have been hit with a more virulent viral strain. The bottom line, however, is that China, along with the East in general, seems better positioned to get on its feet and pick up from where it left off. And while economic weakness in the West impacts China, also true is that China is less dependent on Western markets than in the past.

A specific effect of the pandemic I needed to consider was the unprecedented crash in oil prices as demand cratered and as Saudi Arabia and Russia, for a time, pumped all out in an effort to gain market share. At the low point in March, oil prices actually were negative, meaning that sellers had to pay buyers to take the oil off their hands.

Does this mean that the scarcities in oil and other commodities that I discuss in Chapters 7 and 8, and that I expect to contribute to gold's rise, no longer will occur? I wouldn't draw that conclusion. It may take somewhat longer, but I expect that the underlying trends that I identified will start to emerge as the East looks past the pandemic. There's no reason to think that China will suddenly abandon its Belt and Road Initiative or stop seeking to link and create markets in emerging economies, a major driver of rising demand for commodities. Moreover, now China may offer emerging economies the added attraction of funding health infrastructure creation. Meanwhile, the West, economically weakened, may have a lessened ability to offer itself as a counter to China in countries in the emerging world.

The crash in oil also may seal the fate of the U.S. fracking industry sooner than otherwise. As I discuss in Chapter 9, fracking always was a misguided sideshow, and even with oil prices at $50 a barrel, the industry had never managed to be cash positive. Now the crash in prices has driven some frackers out of business. The upshot is that on the other side of the pandemic, U.S. production will likely drop, significantly reducing global supply.

Relatedly, the dramatic drop in oil prices has forced every major oil company to put capital expenditures on future production on hold, and one of the two major offshore drilling companies has gone bankrupt. This could mean less oil from offshore sources, which the industry generally considers to contain the largest incremental supply.

There's more to say about oil. In Chapter 11, I discuss China's establishment of an Eastern oil benchmark denominated in yuan as a steppingstone to the new monetary reserve system China intends to engineer. The plunge in oil prices has made China more important than ever to Saudi Arabia, with the Saudis almost surely now more open to trading oil for yuan. Anything that weakens the long-standing connection between the dollar and oil, which for decades helped keep the dollar as the world's primary reserve currency, strengthens China's hand in creating a new reserve currency.

Also worth noting: in April, as the pandemic was locking up much of the rest of the world, China was testing a digital currency. As I discuss in Chapter 12, a digital currency will be crucial to a new reserve system.

More generally, the U.S. response to the pandemic may well have bolstered the perception of China and other Eastern countries that it is not in their interest for the dollar to continue as the world's dominant reserve currency. The extraordinary money printing the pandemic unleashed has flooded the United States and the world with dollars. This undermines the very idea of a reserve currency, which is supposed to be something that can allocate scarcities among goods. It reinforces what China saw in 2008–2009, when at first there weren't enough dollars to go around and then there were far too many.

One unfortunate effect of the pandemic has been to sharply intensify the hostility between the United States and China. Both countries
seem to be ever more in the throes of heightened nationalistic fervor
and attempts to blame the other for the pandemic and much else. I
already had bemoaned the emergence of a new cold war mentality
that increasingly seemed to dictate how the United States was viewing
China. I saw this as squandering the best chance to meet the existential
issues the world faces this century, and moreover, I believed that it was
a contest the United States wasn't going to win. To the extent that the
pandemic has further moved us away from a cooperative relationship
between the world's two biggest countries, it only further disadvantages
the United States.

In the original cold war between the United States and the Soviet
Union, the United States had the educational and technologic standing
to prevail. Today the indications are that we're lagging China, including in our management of COVID-19. In the increasingly hostile
competition and rhetoric between China and the United States, a lot
is at stake, including which country will be best positioned to establish the rules of the road in setting the technological standards of the
future. Before the pandemic, I gave China the edge. And now, that
edge seems, if anything, stronger.

In Chapter 19, as emblematic of the U.S. approach, I talk about
U.S. efforts to hem in Huawei, including keeping it out of 5G networks. Before the pandemic, the United States had failed to persuade
even some of its closest allies to go along with us. More recently, I
came across the telling factoid that a major telecom in Canada, Telus,
was using Huawei equipment, which Telus management boasted of to
explain its edge over competitors. This seemed to epitomize the futility
of thinking we can keep China down.

Finally, I want to make what seems to be a necessary disclaimer.
In today's climate, it can seem that giving China credence for doing
anything right, or favorably comparing it with the United States in
any respect, can lead to being called a dupe or a traitor. I'm far from
thinking that China is perfect, and there's much that I deplore about

its government, its legal system, its human rights record, and more. Nothing that I write about China's past achievements or its capabilities going forward means that I'm blind to China's very real flaws.

In the context of looking at how China could affect the world going forward, though, it's not a matter of making moral judgments. It's a question of trying to see as objectively as I can what the evidence and data suggest. And both prepandemic and now, I think that the signs point to China proceeding in ways that are certain to lead to far higher gold prices.

And finally, speaking of gold . . . when the stock market crashed as the pandemic emerged, gold handily outperformed all other assets. This is hardly surprising. We were facing a deflationary cataclysm. As I explain in Chapter 3, gold outperforms both during deflationary periods and during periods of commodity-driven inflation. The only environment hostile for gold is a "Goldilocks" economy, where growth is neither too hot nor too cold but just right ("gold or Goldilocks").

But as the world, or large parts of it centered in the East, moves past the pandemic, the dynamics pushing gold prices higher will shift. Rather than being driven by deflationary fears, the gains will come from commodity scarcities and a new monetary system. This won't happen instantaneously. In fact, there likely will be a period when growth resumes but commodity scarcities aren't yet visible, causing gold to retreat. But that will be a temporary interlude before gold starts making gains that will dwarf anything seen before. The pandemic has thrown a nasty wrench into a lot of lives and destroyed a lot of dreams. But it hasn't destroyed the case for gold, which I believe offers investors the single best path to making up for lost ground.

Acknowledgments

IN VARIOUS WAYS, all the following friends and associates helped me greatly during the course of writing this book. My long-time friend Tom Kaplan shared invaluable insights into gold and gold investing along with his stimulating and at times refreshingly sardonic perspective on world events. Eric King, who runs what I consider the most informative website for all things of interest to gold investors, was a constant source of encouragement and provided a forum for honing and presenting some of my thinking. Al Zuckerman of Writers House, my outstanding agent and friend for more decades than I wish I had to admit to, tactfully and tirelessly prodded me to get the book done. He also connected me to my initial editor at McGraw-Hill, Noah Schwartzberg, to whom I owe enormous gratitude for his receptivity to my ideas and for his patience and empathy during a challenging period. Many thanks as well to Donya Dickerson, our subsequent editor, for seamlessly picking up the reins, and to Joseph Scott Kurtz for his thorough and detailed reading of the manuscript. I also am enormously appreciative of all the support from my associates at my office. In particular, I want to thank Scott Chan, who held down the fort in countless ways with his usual equanimity; Esi Abaidoo, for her "no problem" readiness to step in so competently at all times; and Steve Perkins, for hanging in and showing up and taking care of business through thick and thin. Thanks also go to Aaron Zuckerman for his exceedingly helpful contributions to the chapter on investing in physical gold. Finally, this book would not have been possible if my wife and coauthor Donna Leeb had not agreed to participate, throwing herself into the project with her usual skill and ability to translate my research and thinking into readable prose.

1

Introduction: Get Ready for Gold

A FEW YEARS ago, I became convinced that a powerful bull market in gold would propel the metal to price levels never before seen—at least as high as $20,000 an ounce and possibly well beyond that. I wasn't sure about the precise timing. But I knew that timing was less important than being right about such a bull move ultimately taking place. As an investor, if you can get on the right side of the truly big moves in any market, you've got it made. And this was going to be a truly gargantuan move.

Since then, everything I've seen happening in the world has only added to my conviction that an unprecedented long-term bull market in gold is inevitable. And now I suspect that it will happen sooner rather than later.

The postwar period has seen two major gold bull markets. In the first, between 1971 and 1980, gains in gold averaged a stunning 42 percent a year. The second bull market began in 2001 with gold at $273; by 2011, the metal had reached a high of $1,920 before coming down part of the way. More recently, it has been recovering, in a new up phase that in coming years will gather speed and force—no doubt with corrections along the way—that will ultimately qualify as the greatest bull market ever.

Moreover, the multifold gains I foresee in the metal itself understate the potential opportunities that will open up for investors. Even bigger fortunes will be made by investing in many of the miners and especially in some of the so-called junior miners, that is, smaller companies with reserves but no production, as happened in prior bull markets in gold, when some of the best-situated miners made hundredfold gains.

In the following pages, I explain the events and trends that I see as pointing to massively higher gold prices and explain how you can best benefit. I hope that I can convince you that I'm right because if I do, and if you act on it, I'm confident that you'll be handsomely rewarded.

You will quickly notice that around 99 percent of my thinking revolves around China and the East. In fact, at times, it might seem as if I'm writing (another) book about China. Almost a decade ago, in my last book, *Red Alert*, I wrote about China's rise, its long-term perspective, its accumulation of vital resources, and the way its growth would inevitably challenge the United States, which I saw as deplorably complacent.

Since then, most of what I forecast has been borne out as China's status as a major power and major economy has come into ever clearer focus. In the past decade, China has become increasingly active on numerous fronts, engaging with the world more intensely and purposefully than ever before.

Today, China is ubiquitous. It often seems to dominate the news, whether the focus is on trade wars, human rights, China's activities in the South China Sea, its stance on Hong Kong, or something else. Books about China abound from across the political spectrum, some even suggesting that China–U.S. armed conflict may be inevitable.

From a standing start a couple of decades ago, China has become what is generally termed the world's *second biggest economy*, although actually, by some measures, it's already the biggest. It's unquestionably the world's biggest trader. Whatever you think about China, there's no doubt that today it's a really big deal. Love it or hate it, decry its authoritarian political system or appreciate that it has lifted hundreds of millions of people out of poverty, you can't question that China matters.

But, for all that is being written and said about China, I have yet to see anything that looks at China and whispers: buy gold.

Maybe this is not surprising. For me to arrive at this conclusion, I needed to connect a series of sometimes far-flung and often opaque dots. But as I have studied China's activities and pronouncements and assessed innumerable data points, those connections seemed increasingly clear. China's rise is spearheading a historic shift in economic power from West to East that is leading to a foundational change in global relationships. It's a change that points inexorably to higher gold prices. And the United States will be powerless to hold back the tide.

There are two powerful reasons why China's continued rise as a global economic heavyweight will result in soaring gold prices.

1. **Forthcoming commodity scarcities.** Historically, commodity scarcities go hand in hand with bull markets in gold. Such scarcities will develop as China pushes ahead with its ambitious Belt and Road Initiative (BRI), through which it is investing at least a trillion dollars and likely far more to build up and link developing economies throughout the East and beyond. The effort has now even expanded into the developed world, with Italy being the first Western nation to sign on as a BRI participant.

   The enormous amount of new infrastructure China is creating, within its own borders as well as throughout the developing world, and the economic growth such infrastructure will foster require huge inputs of commodities of all kinds. This ensures that demand for commodities will be rising sharply, leading to scarcities and rising prices. These are conditions that have always led to rising gold prices. Commodity scarcities will constitute one pillar supporting gold's rise.

2. **A new monetary reserve system.** If commodity scarcities were the only factor, I would still expect gold to be a strong performer. But a second development will supercharge gains in the metal. China intends to engineer a new monetary reserve system that will replace or at the very least strongly compete with the global dollar-based system that has prevailed since the end of World War II. This will be transformational.

    It's important to realize that China isn't looking to replace the dollar with its own currency, the yuan. Rather, all signs point to China intending for the new reserve currency to take the form of a basket of currencies backed by gold. Because a relatively fixed amount of gold will underpin an expanding volume of international trade, gold's price inevitably will be pushed higher.

    Note that gold's role in this new reserve currency will be very different from the old gold standard that once prevailed, in which gold was pegged to the dollar at a fixed rate. It's not a return to a system that no longer fits our world. It's a step into a system that will better match the realities of the future.

Can China Swing It?

The case I detail for gold in the pages ahead depends on the health and strength of China's economy and political system. You might wonder if that hasn't become a risky bet.

Will China really have the wherewithal to continue making big investments in infrastructure in the developing world? Will its currency and financial system be strong enough and exhibit enough appeal and transparency to induce the rest of the world to shift from the dollar to some new version of a reserve currency? Even if I'm right about what China wants to do, why am I confident it will be able to carry it off? Why don't I think the United States will be able to stop it, as it would seem to be in America's interests to do?

After all, it might seem as if the United States has woken up with a vengeance to the challenges posed by China. We've slapped tariffs on its exports. We've taken steps to throttle its tech industry, in particular by emasculating China's tech giant Huawei. And in December 2017, the Trump administration released a new National Security Statement that moved away from the idea of mostly cooperating with China and labeled it, along with Russia, a "revisionist" power that had to be confronted. Just in case China gets any ideas about getting into a real fight with us, our defense budget as of 2018 was more than two and a half times China's.

The Western financial press seems never to run out of stories that suggest that China, after years of remarkable growth, is now in trouble. Their gist is that China's growth is slowing. The country is awash in corporate debt. Its banks are burdened by a high level of nonperforming loans. BRI countries have grown disillusioned with China, resenting or even rejecting Chinese investments because of so-called debt traps. Is it really plausible to think China can surmount all these issues?

To answer, I'll offer some words of wisdom from beloved baseball great Yogi Berra. Yogi normally wouldn't figure in a book about China and gold or in any investment book for that matter, but coincidentally, the beloved baseball icon died in September 2015 as Chinese President Xi was making a state visit to the United States, so both Yogi and Xi made headlines the same day. As it happens, one of the many seemingly addled quotes attributed to Yogi resonated strongly with me in relation to China, the United States, and the outlook for gold.

The quote is: "If you don't know where you're going, you'll end up someplace else." China—in contrast to the United States—*does* know where it's going, making it likely that it will get there. It's not that China won't run into setbacks that could delay some steps or force it to change tactics and veer around obstacles. But its history strongly suggests that it will keep its end goals in view and work to get there.

Understanding that China plays the long game is one of the most important insights you can have about what lies ahead. China's leaders know where they want to be five and ten years out. They understand what it will take to get there and are willing to commit the necessary effort and funds. They take steps now that will pay off only further down the line. The country has followed this approach for decades, as far back as the 1970s, when Deng Xiaoping became China's leader.

What China wants above all is to control its own destiny so as to ensure that its economy can grow and provide for the needs of its enormous population as the twenty-first century progresses. Part and parcel of that is making itself immune to what it sees as Western bullying, as well as to the kind of Western carelessness than led to the 2008 financial crisis, which had a deep impact on China. China is moving to create the conditions that will ensure that it has vibrant markets and trading partners and access to resources and that no other country will be able to thwart its achieving what Chinese President Xi calls "the Chinese dream." And I would caution against misinterpreting the word *dream*.

In later chapters I'll address in detail the various issues that have been raised about China's growth and debt and all the rest. But here's a spoiler alert: nothing suggests to me that China will be derailed. And that means gold prices will rise.

America's Role

Gold's rise will reflect at least in part what I see as America's decline over the past half century. That decline stems in large part from our focus on short-term gratification, which stands in sharp contrast to China's ability to plan for the long term.

If the United States had gone down a different road in its own fiscal and domestic policies, we likely would be less vulnerable today to China and its ambitions, including China's determination to promote gold. In turn, gold's rise will further exacerbate America's decline by taking power away from the dollar. This will undermine America's ability to work its will in the world and could lead to a fair amount of economic turmoil here.

What should America do? For starters, instead of seeking to shut down China's progress—Huawei springs to mind—it would serve us better to devote the resources and dedication needed to improve the fundamentals of our own society and economy. We could begin with a huge investment in infrastructure, for example, including renewable energy.

I also think that it would be in our interests to dial back on the confrontational approach toward China we've adopted and that both political parties here are now largely embracing. As China forges ahead, there will be areas where the two countries can work more productively together. If we view China merely as an enemy and see our relationship as a zero-sum game, we risk missing out on opportunities for cooperation that could set our own country on a stronger path.

There is still time—not a lot, but some—for the United States to make a course correction that could improve its outlook as the twenty-first century proceeds. It's essential, though, that we see the world not as it once was, not as we might wish it still were, but as it actually is. It's a world in which the East, led by China, is going to have a lot more say. We need to respond to this reality with intelligence, not bluster.

A final comment: as you read through the following chapters, I hope that you won't think that I am naively viewing China through rose-tinted glasses and ignoring all the things in China that are troublesome. There's plenty in China to criticize, plenty that I don't like. I am not sugar-coating any of it. But my purpose in writing this book isn't to make value judgments or to bemoan reality. It is to present reality, to lay out what I see as the key trends in the world today, and explain what they mean for investors.

China's rise is changing the world in any number of ways that historians will be chronicling for a long time to come. I can't predict all the ramifications of China's rise, but I can confidently predict that for historians who trace the financial markets, the biggest financial story of the coming decade and beyond will be the connection between China's ascension and gold's coming glory. So far, though, it's a connection that has gotten virtually no attention. Meanwhile, buying gold will likely be the best way, even perhaps the only way, that most Americans can secure their financial future in a world that will be marked by historic change.

2
Why Americans Shun Gold

IN THE SPRING of 2017, I attended a lovely dinner party honoring a friend's daughter who had recently gotten married. The bride's mother made a point of introducing me to a relative-by-marriage who was quite prominent in the investment world, figuring that he and I would have a lot in common and enjoy talking to each other.

Well, not exactly. Both of us eschewing small talk, we dove right into presenting our views on where the world and financial markets were headed. I told him why I thought gold would be embarking on a huge and sustained bull market, one presenting the biggest opportunity for investors in many generations, perhaps ever. And he told me why I was a total idiot.

Specifically, he told me in no uncertain terms that the dollar would remain king for a long time to come. Gold would continue to play virtually no role as a monetary currency. China was struggling with mountains of debt and, contrary to what I had contended, was in no position to engineer a new monetary system centered on gold. Investors should keep buying the kinds of financial assets, like stocks, that had been soaring. In short, I was wrong on everything I had so confidently asserted.

If I was disappointed in my hopes of finding a kindred spirit, I can't say that I was shocked by his reaction. He was only saying what the great majority of financial actors and commentators in this country believe. Still, the encounter drove home for me several things (besides the thought that perhaps I should stick to small talk at social gatherings).

It illuminated for me the blindness—what I see as partly a willful blindness—by the U.S. financial elite to how profoundly America's position in the world is changing. Relatedly, it made it plain that the financial elite has a surprisingly superficial understanding of what China is all about. Put these two realities together, and it's no wonder that American financiers are so dismissive of the possibility that the dollar's top-dog position may be in its final days.

China, for its part, is far closer than financiers here imagine to replacing the existing global monetary system with something new. This new system will be linked to gold, which will be one of several developments leading to a sharp rise in the metal's price. And unless something changes in how Americans view gold, most Americans will miss out on those gains, as most missed out in the past when gold has risen.

Americans have been conditioned to overlook gold as an asset class that under certain circumstances cries out to constitute a significant portion of their investment portfolio. Before getting to the meat of this book, which is to set forth all the reasons that point to a historic rise in gold prices, it's worth looking at why Americans have typically stayed away from the metal. If you're going to be among those who confidently jump in and buy, you will likely need to stand your ground against the many naysayers who will earnestly try to steer you every which way but toward gold.

Self-Interest Wins Every Time

You may have noticed, a couple of paragraphs up, my use of the word *willful*. In resisting the idea that the dollar's status is at risk, not in some far-off future but perhaps within the next couple of years, American financiers aren't simply ill-informed, nor would I ever say that they are stupid people. Rather, as elites generally do, they have an instinctive tendency to push back against even the idea of anything that could force them to give up privileges that they have long enjoyed and consider their due.

The American financial class has benefited hugely from the dollar remaining the world's primary reserve currency, which it continued to be even after Nixon delinked the dollar from gold in 1971. That step had a multitude of pernicious repercussions. I look at many of them in later chapters when I discuss how the United States began going astray during the last century in ways that make us vulnerable today to China's ambitions.

Here I'll point out just one of those unfortunate repercussions: the finance sector became a disproportionately large—and largely unproductive—part of the overall U.S. economy. This happened because once the dollar no longer was linked to gold, dollars could be, and were, printed with abandon to pay for whatever seemed like a good idea at the time. This helped fuel the emergence of a financial class that was paid huge amounts of money to manage those dollars. Aided and abetted by increasingly fast computers, members of the financial elite developed ever more creative, complex, and lucrative (for them) ways to make money by promoting dollar-based assets.

The health and wealth of corporations in this country, and of the people who invest in them and run them, and of the banks that finance the companies' public offerings, not to mention the lawyers devoted to handling the massive amounts of paperwork generated by all these activities, are built around the primacy of the dollar. Take that away, and you've started to pull the rug out from under the entire edifice.

So far the dollar has remained a reliable underpinning for that edifice. This is because, as the primary global reserve currency, it is always in demand. If you're a country that wants to conduct trade with other countries (and what country doesn't), you need dollars. Particularly important, if you want to buy oil and other commodities, you need dollars. This reality has kept the financial class happily afloat (in some cases literally so on the yachts that are among the perks they choose to reward themselves with). It's also what has given the United States the power to impose sanctions so freely on any country it deems an enemy or wants to punish for some infraction or other.

But if the dollar had to compete in a serious way as a currency with something else, it would be a different story. And if that something else were linked to gold, the threads would unravel particularly quickly—especially when it came to the trading of oil and other commodities and even more so if such commodities were facing scarcities. Under such circumstances, producers of commodities would like nothing more than to exchange them for gold, or for a currency linked to gold, rather than for a fiat currency such as the dollar that can be printed at will. The dollar might still maintain a significant role in global trade, but if it had to compete with a gold-linked alternative, it would be far less dominant than it is now as demand for dollars inevitably lessened.

No wonder the financial class in the United States has pushed to keep gold from assuming—or, more accurately, reassuming—a role as a bona fide currency.

The Strange Case of BIS

The Bank of International Settlements (BIS), headquartered in Basel, Switzerland, is known as the central bank for central banks. It's one of the most powerful institutions you've likely never heard of. Founded in 1930, its mission is to ensure international monetary and financial stability.

One of its responsibilities is to ensure that banks have enough protection available to deal with any crisis that might erupt. This means having a sufficient amount of liquid assets on hand, assets that can be depended on to maintain their value under even the most tumultuous circumstances. Defining such assets is an important part of what BIS does. U.S. Treasury bills are always a big part of the mix. Other highly liquid assets include AAA-rated sovereign debt.

The catastrophic 2008–2009 financial crisis made it obvious that BIS needed to raise the standards relating to liquidity to forestall any repetition of that financial meltdown. During the worst of that crisis, banks were left so high and dry that General Electric nearly missed a payroll because it did not have access to enough liquidity. Specifically, BIS set out to ensure that banks would have a buffer large enough to cover net bank withdrawals over an extremely stressful 30-day period. It issued its new guidelines, known as *Basel III*, in 2013.

It had been widely assumed that BIS would include gold as a financial asset banks could use to constitute part of their liquidity. Amazingly, though, when BIS issued its recommendations (the guidelines are voluntary, but banks take them very seriously), gold was nowhere to be found. What was on the list? Acceptable forms of liquidity included sovereign debt, common stocks, and BBB+ bonds (some with a *haircut*, i.e., at less than full face value).

That decision to snub gold in 2013 was extraordinary. On any logical grounds, omitting gold made no sense given gold's outstanding performance during the worst of times in this century's first decade. Between the start of the Great Recession on September 30, 2007 through March 6, 2009, when the market bottomed, gold gained 26 percent. This left every other asset in the dust. Only long-dated U.S. Treasuries came close. Germany's 30-year note lost about 20 percent, whereas Britain's 20-year bond lost about 40 percent. The Standard and Poor's 500 Index (S&P 500) lost over 55 percent. Furthermore, only U.S. bonds were less volatile than gold.

In other words, by any objective measure, gold would have been far and away the most suitable liquidity buffer of all. Yet BIS left it out entirely in favor of common stocks and mediocre bonds. BIS's actions contributed to the price of gold sinking from $1,800 an ounce in October 2012 to below $1,200 by the end of June 2013, a 35 percent plunge in a mere eight months. The downtrend continued until the end of 2015, when gold briefly traded below $1,050.

BIS's inexplicable decision to ignore gold only makes sense when you realize how desperate Western financial elites have been to prevent gold from being recognized as a currency. If gold resumed a role as an acknowledged currency, central bankers in the United States and Europe could no longer control monetary policy by printing money, as the U.S. Federal Reserve did through its quantitative easing program. Printing more dollars, or more of any paper currency, would simply make that currency ever less valuable relative to the one currency of which there was a fixed amount, that is, gold.

Gold's value would rise in proportion to the amount of paper money that was newly printed. In the most extreme case, that money would literally be worth only the paper it was printed on. Goods and services would be denominated in gold, and printing more money would resemble a dog chasing its tail. Control of the economy would pass to whoever held the most gold, blowing apart the world economy's monetary foundations.

BIS's action isn't the only example this decade of the West fighting gold as a currency. Another came a short time later when Cyprus, in the midst of a severe financial crisis, sought help from the International Monetary Fund (IMF) and European Commission (EC). What did those bodies do? They imposed severe requirements that, astoundingly, allowed Cyprus to confiscate money from individuals' savings accounts—while ordering Cyprus to sell its gold reserves to raise cash as a contribution to the bailout. Cyprus ultimately resisted, but the message was clear: the West, regardless of the circumstances, was unwilling to admit that gold could be a primary asset. Rather, gold was treated merely as a way to obtain putatively more important monetary assets, such as sovereign bonds, dollars, and euros.

BIS in 2019

But that isn't the end of the story. BIS regularly updates its guidelines in lengthy and somewhat obscure monthly reports. In March of 2019, BIS very quietly reversed its 2013 stance on gold as a monetary asset banks could hold to satisfy liquidity requirements.

Assets that are coveted for liquidity are those with zero risk or close to zero risk. To achieve 0 percent risk, an asset must satisfy various criteria—for instance, it has to be present in sufficient quantities, it must be actively traded, and transaction costs should be relatively low. In addition, its price should not be unduly influenced by its need as a liquidity buffer.

The relevant passage in the updated guidelines—buried deep within the report—is found in the following sentences: "i) a 0% risk weight will apply to cash owned and held at the bank . . . and ii) gold bullion held at the bank." In other words, when it comes to risk-weighted assets, BIS had decided to view gold and cash as equals. This was a huge change, finally elevating to reality what everyone had presumed would occur in the regulations that followed the 2008 crisis.

What led BIS to do such an about-face? I think it had real concerns that the world economy was on tenuous footing and that it couldn't mess around. By assigning gold a zero-risk rating, BIS was encouraging central banks to hold gold, which, if the dollar were to come under pressure, might be the one thing that would keep banks solvent.

BIS's reversal hasn't gotten much attention, and the financial elite in the West is still far from willing to give much sway to gold as a monetary metal. But it can be seen as an important harbinger, signifying that in the future, resisting gold will become ever more difficult. And if central bankers increase their demand for gold, it adds one more reason to expect a bull market in gold that will dwarf anything seen before.

Et Tu, Buffett

We can't discuss the Western financial elite's long-time disdain for gold without bringing in Warren Buffett. Buffett is justly known as one of capitalism's all-time great investors, and he's one of capitalism's most ardent boosters.

He also is known for his scorn for gold, which, quoting John Maynard Keynes, he has termed a "barbarous" investment. One of

Buffett's well-known screeds against the metal points out that all the gold in the world could be melted down into a cube measuring around 68 feet per side. At gold's price at the time of this observation, that cube would have been worth around $9.6 trillion. Buffett asks, as if it were a rhetorical question, why anyone would rationally prefer to own that cube, which just sits there and does nothing productive, when the same $9.6 trillion would have bought all U.S. cropland plus 16 ExxonMobils, with a handy $1 trillion left over as pocket change.

On inspection, however, Buffett's argument falls down for lack of logic. If gold were a currency, you could take the gold making up that cube and use it to buy farmland or oil companies or anything else, just as right now you could do with dollars. You could just as well rephrase Buffett's question to ask what would you rather have, all the dollar bills in the world piled together in a gigantic multi-mile-high pile or farmland and oil companies.

The satirical paper *The Onion* makes the point better than I can. In February 2010, it ran an article reporting on supposed testimony by then Federal Reserve Chairman Ben Bernanke before a Senate committee. Under the headline, "U.S. Economy Grinds to a Halt as Nation Realizes Money Is Just a Symbolic, Mutually Shared Illusion," the article began

> The U.S. economy ceased to function this week after unexpected existential remarks by Federal Reserve Chairman Ben Bernanke shocked Americans into realizing that money is, in fact, just a meaningless and intangible social construct.
>
> What began as a routine report before the Senate Finance Committee Tuesday ended with Bernanke passionately disavowing the entire concept of currency, and negating in an instant the very foundation of the world's largest economy.

Money, in other words, like religion, is based on faith. Whether you're talking about gold or dollar bills or, for that matter, wampum, it comes down to the need to have faith in a medium of exchange that in itself is essentially useless and unproductive. You *use* money to buy things that are useful or productive. Producers of those things accept money because they have faith that they'll be able to use it to get something they want.

And when it comes to faith, gold has it all over the dollar. It has a far longer history as a currency. Unlike the dollar and other paper money, it can't be printed at will. It possesses unique physical characteristics that have made it prized throughout the centuries.

In his professed disdain for gold, we think that Buffett, who understands the implications of permitting gold to be viewed as a currency, has been disingenuous. After all, in the 1980s, Buffett was the largest single holder of another precious metal, silver. Since Buffett's case against gold clearly would be comparably apt with respect to silver, there's a logical inconsistency to his ranting about gold. Once it became public knowledge that Buffett was accumulating silver, he stopped reporting his holdings. Presumably at some point he sold. But his willingness at the time to hold massive amounts of silver doesn't suggest someone who thinks owning precious metals is inherently nonsensical or barbarous.

More likely is that Buffett has been engaging in what in the financial trade is known as "talking his book"—presenting the arguments best suited to protecting his own interests. Anything that would bolster the case for gold gaining status as a currency would threaten the dollar, American capitalism, and Buffett's empire. Like virtually every Western banker, from J. P. Morgan to the central bankers who run BIS, Buffett counts his money in dollars, making him understandably wary of anything that would upset the dollar's hegemony.

Your Friendly, Ill-Informed Financial Planner

It's not just the financial world's big guns like Buffett with a self-interest in dollar-based assets who have contributed to steering most investors away from gold. The attitude permeates lower down the financial food chain. It's ingrained in those who have the greatest personal contact with individual Americans striving to make sense of their finances so as to obtain some security for themselves and their families.

I'm referring to certified financial planners (CFPs). Many Americans rely on these professionals for guidance with their financial affairs. And don't get me wrong, I'm not knocking CFPs. They can be exceedingly helpful. To receive certification, they study an extensive curriculum and must pass rigorous exams covering a wide range of topics. They can help Americans make intelligent, informed decisions on everything from putting money aside for their children's education to figuring out how big a house they can afford.

Unfortunately, though, one thing they lack is an understanding of what propels bull markets in gold. Finding a CFP who will recommend that you buy gold is as likely as finding a butcher who will urge you to go vegan. The investment portion of the CFP curriculum constitutes just a small part of the overall course, and gold makes up a minuscule portion of that investment section. When it comes to advising their clients on investments, CFPs have a limited and increasingly outdated perspective. The books they study in order to pass the CFP exam pay scant attention to gold, which is treated as essentially a taboo investment that should be avoided. And CFPs have little familiarity with various ways to buy gold.

Instead, the traditional advice from financial planners is to invest in a mix of stocks, funds, and bonds, with the bond portion increasing as retirement nears. Gold and other precious metals are shunned as supposedly volatile, non-income-producing assets. At best, CFPs might grudgingly agree that investors who harbor fears of some coming cataclysm might devote a very small portion of their assets, 1 or 2 percent, to precious metals, simply for some peace of mind.

If this approach ever made sense, it doesn't any more. When it comes to gold, China's rise has fundamentally changed the calculus. At some point, CFPs will catch on and catch up. For now, though, they're still mired in the past, which could leave many American families on the sidelines as gold soars.

In China, the attitude toward investing in gold is very different. Today, anyone in China can walk into a bank and purchase gold, which is available in denominations small enough to be a feasible purchase for all but the poorest Chinese citizens. Until 2002, it had actually been illegal for Chinese citizens to own gold other than as jewelry. By the fall of 2009, however, the government had begun aggressively urging consumers to buy gold and other precious metals as an investment, even running programs about gold investing on state-owned television.

By 2014, according to an interview Bloomberg conducted with Albert Cheng, then the World Gold Council's managing director for the Far East, 100,000 bank branches in China offered gold—which, Cheng noted, compared to a total of 50,000 outlets in the United States for Starbucks, McDonald's, and Subway combined.

Chinese citizens have responded enthusiastically and have taken to investing in gold in rising amounts. As a result, higher gold prices will add greatly to their wealth in coming years. This plays hand in glove with the government's goal of making China's economy more consumer driven. In fact, it's not farfetched to think that one reason China's government has encouraged gold investing is that it is convinced that gold will be rising, and one reason for that conviction is that it knows that its own actions—including making gold part of a new monetary system—will lead to higher gold prices.

In the United States, while there are lots of ways to invest in gold, it's not something the typical U.S. consumer can casually obtain. If you walked into a branch of Citibank or Chase and asked to buy gold, the teller would look at you as if you were nuts—as if you had asked to buy smoked salmon with a bagel and cream cheese on the side.

Speaking of nuts, I want to make one disclaimer here: I am not, and never have been, what's known as a "gold bug." This is the somewhat derisive term used to describe a group of gold aficionados who are chronic boosters of the metal, seemingly *always* arguing that gold is the one investment to own. They are frequently viewed as nutty.

For much of my time as an investment adviser, I have shunned gold because, under many circumstances, gold is a terrible investment. Under other circumstances, though, gold has been a spectacular performer. The trick is to understand the difference and to be in gold when the circumstances are right.

3
Two Bull Markets in Gold

SINCE THE END of World War II, there have been two great bull markets in gold—the second of which remains ongoing today, with much stronger gains ahead. Separating the two was a long stretch of years in which gold was a dud. And within each gold bull market were stretches of time when gold fell for a while before heading back up. All these periods, bull and bear alike, offer lessons about investing in gold.

Lesson number 1 is gold's connection to commodities. More specifically, commodity scarcities. More specifically still, the possibility of commodity scarcities that could persist over the long term. Scarcities or the threat of scarcities in essential resources such as oil, copper, zinc, silver, and others go hand in hand with rising gold prices.

The reason is that when commodity scarcities arise and look like they could persist and intensify, with no clear end in sight, gold is pushed up to the plate as the one asset capable of allocating those scarcities. Gold is a natural choice for this vital role. It's an asset with universal credibility, something that everyone everywhere is happy to accept. Although it's a commodity itself, gold's special qualities set it apart from other commodities and make it perfectly suited to serve as a currency, something other commodities are ill equipped to do (silver is a partial exception). When commodity scarcities thrust gold into this role, gold prices rise faster and higher than prices of other commodities.

A second lesson is that gold bull markets, like bull markets in stocks or any other asset, will have dips or corrections. Nothing goes straight up. But understanding the fundamentals that underlie a bull market in gold can keep you from panicking and bailing out too soon. Of course, if you can perfectly time every dip and every move back up, so much the better. But if you possessed that kind of ability, you wouldn't need to be reading this or any book about investing. You'd be retired on some gorgeous island and making fun of relative paupers like Jeff Bezos and Bill Gates.

Returning to the real world, a third lesson is that when gold is good, it's very good. You don't want to miss out. If you stick with a more typical stock market portfolio, unless you're preternaturally talented at stock picking, whatever gains you make are likely to look depressingly pallid compared with what you'd have gained with gold.

A fourth message is that we are now in the midst of a bull market in gold that started more than a decade and a half ago and is nowhere near over. However, for much of the investing public, it's a bull market that has occurred under the radar. In the last few years, much gushing attention has been lavished on the performance of the stock market because the Dow Jones Industrial Average topped 27,000 in 2019 and the broader-based Standard and Poor's 500 Index (S&P 500) climbed past 3,000. But that's nothing compared to gold's rise.

Just consider that from the start of this century through August 2019, the gains in the S&P 500 (including dividends) were a bit above 200 percent. Gold's gains over the same time? They were 419 percent.

This is a remarkable showing. Almost equally remarkable, though, is how few investors are aware of it, reflecting the tendency of U.S. investors and their advisers to largely overlook gold. Tracing in some detail the two postwar bull markets in gold offers insight into gold's potential in coming years.

Normalized as of 12/31/1999
Last Price
····· SPXT Index 304.59
—— XAU Curncy 525.33

525.33 Gold Spot

304.59 S&P 500

| 2000 | 2001 | 2002 | 2003 | 2004 | 2005 | 2006 | 2007 | 2008 | 2009 | 2010 | 2011 | 2012 | 2013 | 2014 | 2015 | 2016 | 2017 | 2018 | 2019 |

FIGURE 3.1   Performance of gold (XAU) vs. S&P 500 2000–2019
Source: Bloomberg

Bull Market Number 1

The first postwar bull market in gold—one of the greatest bull markets in any asset ever—was kicked off after President Nixon delinked gold from the dollar in August 1971. Until then, for the two and a half decades following the 1944 Bretton Woods Conference that established the postwar monetary order, gold had been pegged to the dollar at a price of $35 per ounce.

From its lowly start (which, to be precise, was actually $40 an ounce, not $35, because traders in London had bumped the price up in anticipation of Nixon's move), gold topped out near $850 an ounce in early 1980. This is a stunning twentyfold gain that works out to an equally stunning average annual gain of 42 percent a year.

How does this compare with the performance of the stock market over the same period? Total returns (including dividends) for the S&P 500 were around 65 percent. Scorecard: annualized gains of 6.1 percent for stocks versus 42 percent for gold.

This already gaping differential actually understates the true gap in returns. During those years, inflation, as measured by the Consumer Price Index (CPI), rose by more than 93 percent, an annualized rate of

8.1 percent. So the more valid comparison is that if you had put your money into gold in 1971 and held it until early 1980, you'd have made more than 32 percent a year after inflation versus *losing* about 2 percent a year in stocks. This should whet your appetite for being in gold at the right time.

There are a few other things you need to know about the bull market in gold in the 1970s. One is that Americans couldn't join the party until 1975, by which time gold already had more than quadrupled in price to around $200 an ounce. This was because since 1933, it had been largely illegal for Americans to own gold bullion or coins. President Franklin Roosevelt imposed the ban in April of 1933, shortly after taking office, as part of his effort to tackle the Great Depression. Americans who owned gold were required to hand it in to banks by May 1 in exchange for $20.67 in paper money per ounce of gold. Failure to do so was a criminal act punishable by up to 10 years in prison. (There were some exceptions; dentists, for instance, were allowed to own up to 100 ounces of gold, and gold jewelry wasn't affected by the ban.)

The ban was lifted on January 1, 1975, after President Gerald Ford signed a bill Congress had passed repealing the 1933 act. Gold was then trading near $185 an ounce. But Americans who plunged into gold the moment they were permitted to do so probably initially regretted that decision. That's because gold corrected sharply, falling to a low of around $100 an ounce by mid-1976. Some gold investors undoubtedly held on for a while, only to get shaken out of the metal near its low point.

American investors who held onto their gold, however, ended up with a smile. Starting in mid-1976, gold embarked on the second and final upleg of the 1970s' bull market that culminated in a price of $850 an ounce on January 21, 1980. The investor who bought gold only to watch it plunge by nearly 50 percent before turning upward still would have realized a fourfold gain by early 1980, one indication of how powerful that bull market was. A somewhat luckier investor who bought the yellow metal at its low of around $100 an ounce in mid-1976 would have realized an eightfold gain.

In short, the 1970s belonged to gold. It was the single best investment you could have made during that decade. (We're excluding anyone who bought a dirt-encrusted picture for pennies at a tag sale thinking the frame might come in handy and found out it was a Picasso. There's investing and then there's luck.) The decade epitomized the truth that when circumstances are right, you really, really, really want to own gold.

Commodities in the 1970s

Chief among those right circumstances are commodity scarcities and rising commodity prices. In the first upleg of the 1970s' gold bull market, commodities were on a tear. One factor was the Vietnam War, which created enormous demand for materials of all kinds needed to service military operations. As the war dragged on with no end in sight, it fanned concern and uncertainty over whether supplies would be sufficient to meet this rising demand. Another factor was the oil embargo imposed by OPEC (the Organization of Petroleum Exporting States) in October 1973 to punish the United States for its support of Israel in the Yom Kippur War. By March 1974, when the embargo ended, oil prices had gone from $3 a barrel to nearly $12 globally and significantly higher in the United States. Other commodities were rising sharply as well.

When gold began to correct in 1975, oil prices had been leveling off after Nixon forged a deal with the Saudis that launched the petrodollar era. Under that arrangement, the Saudis agreed to price their oil in dollars, ensuring that countries around the world would need dollars to buy Saudi oil. In exchange, the United States promised to provide a military shield protecting the Saudi Arabian kingdom against all enemies.

The moderation in oil's uptrend helped the West recover from the stagflation of 1974. And that, in turn, meant that as the world entered 1975, gold faced a cooling off of the inflationary pressures that had spurred its gains from 1971 to the end of 1974.

The dance between gold and commodities continued during gold's second upleg, between 1976 and early 1980. This upleg was catalyzed in part by another Mideast event, the war between Iran and Iraq, which led to another surge in oil and other commodities.

In other words, both uplegs of the 1970s' gold bull market went along with commodity scarcities that at the time had no clear end in sight. The decade overall was marked by strong gains both in gold and in most other commodities, particularly oil. But gold's gains far outstripped those in any other commodity. Industrial metals, for instance, tripled. This was a great showing, but it still amounted to just 15 percent of gold's gains. The commodity that came closest was oil, which rose about 10-fold—still only about half as much as gold's rise.

This points to the general rule, referenced earlier, that when commodity scarcities emerge, especially ones involving oil, prices of all other commodities will rise—but gold prices will rise significantly more. This occurs because gold is the ultimate currency, the only currency that can serve to ration scarce commodities.

Gold's Drought

The 1980s and 1990s brought a very different story. They made it equally plain that when circumstances are wrong, the last thing you want to own is gold. After its peak in early 1980, gold crashed. By late June 1983, it had come all the way back down to $300 an ounce.

Throughout the 1980s and until 1997, gold traded at between $300 and $500 an ounce. Then things got worse. In 1997, gold broke below $300 and stayed below it. On August 27, 1999, it reached a low of $252 an ounce. For the next two years, while never dropping below this level and occasionally staging a small gain, gold essentially treaded water.

If commodity scarcities were the common theme when gold was uptrending, how were commodities behaving during this long drought in gold, stretching between 1980 and December 2001? In the end, after occasional bouts of sound and fury, commodities were essentially trendless. In late 2001, just before gold was at the starting gate of its new bull move, raw industrial prices were close to generational lows. Oil was trading at around $20 a barrel, near its average of the prior two decades.

But this doesn't mean that commodities never went up during that period. Those years had their share of economic shocks. For instance, oil prices nearly doubled between 1986 and 1987, while raw industrial commodities climbed nearly 35 percent. But that wasn't enough to push up gold, which managed only to flirt with the top end of its trading range near the mid-$400s.

Why didn't investors rush into gold during those spikes in commodities? Because the market didn't sense that there was a threat of long-term commodity scarcities. The major reason for oil's surge in 1986–1987 was that OPEC reversed its prior policy of all-out pumping, which had caused prices to drop. Once the cartel decided to pump less generously, prices rose. But the rise reflected the cartel's decision to make adjustments to the match between supply and demand, not inadequate supply.

Another geopolitical event, the first Iraq war, which the United States initiated in 1991 in response to Saddam Hussein's invasion and annexation of Kuwait, also didn't raise fears of a major prolonged impact on oil supply. The market judged that the United States had the situation well in hand, an assessment that proved correct. The war ended after five weeks of air bombardment and 100 hours of troops on the ground, and after a brief surge, oil prices came back down. Meanwhile, gold traded in the middle to low $300s.

During the 1980s and 1990s, as gold dropped and then essentially treaded water at its newly low levels, stocks ended the millennium with one of their best runs ever. Between the S&P 500's low in August 1982 and its high in March 2000, total returns climbed by more than 24-fold. This works out to an average annualized gain of nearly 20 percent.

Bull Market Number 2

As 2001 was drawing to a close, gold entered an extraordinary second bull market. This is the one that has persisted to the present day, albeit, like the first one, with periods of sharp downturn. And it is nowhere near over.

On November 30, 2001, less than two weeks before China was formally admitted to the World Trade Organization (WTO), gold closed at $273 an ounce, and while it didn't start moving seriously higher for a while, it never dropped below that level. Eventually, it began to move up in a big way, in the first upleg of the second postwar gold bull market.

By Saint Patrick's Day 2008, a Monday, gold was trading above $1,000 an ounce. During the week, it hit a high of $1,033. But it closed the week at $920. This was the start of its first real setback since beginning its ascent.

The backdrop, of course, was a world in turmoil, including the collapse of Lehman Brothers and the onset of the Great Recession. During that time, corporations were in desperate need of liquidity, and they were desperate to get dollars. This led major investment banks to sell gold they had on hand simply to raise dollars. At the same time, commodities were coming down sharply. It all combined to bring gold down.

The decline lasted a bit more than half a year. The low came at $681 during the week that began October 20. Gold closed the week on October 24 at $729. This marked the start of a new and powerful upleg that carried gold to a high of $1,920 in early September 2011.

Then it dropped, getting as low as $1,530 in June 2012. It seemed to right itself after that, rising to $1,800 by October of that year. But the upward momentum failed to hold, and gold began a multiyear correction that didn't end until December 2015, when it closed just above $1,000 an ounce. Since then, proceeding in fits and starts, gold has been in a strong overall uptrend, one that has brought it, at the present time, to more than $1,500 an ounce.

As with the first gold bull market, there's a significant tie-in between gold and commodities. I don't think that it's coincidental that gold bottomed as China was joining the WTO. Investors, correctly, had assessed that once China joined the WTO, there would be no holding back this emerging economic powerhouse. China's growth foretold large future demand for commodities. And indeed, gold's initial upleg coincided with sharp gains in commodities, with everything from copper to corn soaring to record highs.

But I believe that this time around the uptrend in commodities has exhibited a qualitatively different nature from their rise in the 1970s. In this century, the outlook for commodities no longer depends on scarcities stemming from ultimately evanescent political events such as the Vietnam War. With China's rise, fundamental scarcities have come into view.

One telling sign of this can be seen in how commodities acted in the wake of the 2008–2009 financial crisis. Not surprisingly, commodities dropped sharply, as did every major asset class but bonds. It is striking, though, that even at their lowest points, in the midst of the worst economic carnage since the Great Depression, every major commodity was trading above its *average* price of the 1990s. The message is that by the middle of the 2000s, even during the Great Recession when demand had sharply receded, it no longer was a given that there always would be enough commodities to go around.

What about the second upleg of the 2000s' bull market, which started in 2015? Between the end of 2015 and early 2016, raw industrials and oil both bottomed and then rose fairly steadily until trade tensions broke out in early to mid-2018. Since then, as of this writing, both are holding well above their 2015–2016 lows despite the worsening tit-for-tat tariffs between the United States and China that have cut projections for global growth to the lowest level since the end of the Great Recession.

That gold has maintained its upward trajectory in the face of lower projections for global growth can be interpreted in two opposite ways. On the one hand, it could mean that the metal is signaling that the trade war will be resolved, allowing global growth to pick up and demand for commodities to rise. This is the inflationary scenario.

On the other hand, it could signal that gold investors are seeking a haven in fear that the trade war will send the world into a deflationary spiral. I lean strongly toward the first interpretation. But gold (see below) is both a deflationary and an inflationary hedge, and the current period clearly points up this dual nature.

Why Gold Is Special

I can't close this chapter without tackling a question whose answer isn't as obvious as it might seem: Why gold? What makes it so special? Why does it lead the pack when other commodities face scarcities (and during other times of economic stress as well)? What does gold have that nothing else does that makes it an ideal choice as a monetary metal?

With apologies to Elizabeth Barrett Browning, let me count the ways. It starts with the fact that other commodities, such as copper and aluminum, are workhorses with a multitude of practical uses. We need them to conduct heat and electricity, to protect buildings against the elements, to make cookware and electronic devices, to store energy. Apart from their ability to do these things, they have no particular appeal. They have no intrinsic value above and beyond their industrial chops. No one opening a little robin's-egg-blue box would be pleased to discover a bangle or ring made of zinc or aluminum.

Other commodities are priced according to an assessment that takes into account both their utility and their scarcity. Copper, for example, is a better conductor of both electricity and thermal energy than aluminum. This makes it more desirable than aluminum. On the other hand, aluminum is much less scarce and therefore cheaper, so there are tradeoffs. If the differences in conductivity are significant enough in a particular application, users will pay up for copper. Otherwise, they might settle for aluminum.

While gold does have a few industrial applications, they all can be satisfied, and generally better, by other commodities. There is nothing that gold does uniquely well when it comes to practical uses, and only about 10 percent of the gold that has been mined has gone to industrial purposes. Gold is valued not for what it does but for what it is. This is a crucial distinction.

This difference leads to two others that make gold ideal as a currency. First, gold is the only commodity that exists largely in a fixed amount. As they are put to work in industry, other commodities get used up, and while some recycling occurs, a lot gets lost. Meanwhile, varying amounts are being mined depending on demand and price. The amount that's present on the face of the Earth isn't fixed, and there's no way to know how much of any commodity is in the world at any one time.

With gold, it's a different story. Gold doesn't get used up. And while gold mining continues to take place, in broad terms the amount of gold being added is relatively small compared with the amount already mined. Essentially nearly all the gold in the world already has been mined and is still present on the face of the Earth. More than any other commodity, gold's value depends solely on demand.

Relatedly, gold's lack of particular utility in industry means that when it's used as a monetary metal, it doesn't detract from economic activity. It's not removing a resource needed for growth.

There's a lot more to say about what makes gold ideal as a monetary metal. It is scarce but not overly rare. It can be found throughout the globe. It is essentially indestructible, neither corroding nor decomposing. Because it isn't subject to oxidation, it doesn't tarnish. It is fungible, meaning that one ounce of gold is identical to any other ounce. It is relatively easy to transport, and it's malleable, able to be subdivided into any unit that convenience requires. Moreover, it can't be artificially produced.

Gold also is simply intrinsically beautiful—perhaps a subjective sort of judgment but one that humans have consistently made throughout history, across continents and civilizations. Gold artifacts date back 6,000–7,000 years. Gold jewelry has been prized pretty much forever.

And, of course, gold's hold on the human imagination is reflected in language, myth, and fairy tales—Rumpelstiltskin seeking to spin straw into gold, the goose that laid the golden egg, silence is golden, golden agers, Olympics gold, good as gold, the golden mean, and on and on.

Gold's unique collection of qualities explains why people turn to gold when for any reason they grow fearful about the economy's future and in particular about the continued availability of essential resources, which are the bedrock of economies. When commodities such as oil, copper, iron ore, and others grow scarcer and more expensive, producers want to make sure that they don't get ripped off or short-changed when they sell them. They become wary about selling them for paper currencies that can be printed at will, losing value. The producers want to get something in exchange that they can depend on to hold its value. Gold, for all the reasons just cited, fits the bill better than anything else.

Deflation, Too

I've just spent the last few thousand words linking sharp gains in gold with rising commodities, which is another way of saying rising inflation. This is in line with the common view of gold as a quintessential inflation hedge, which it can be. But that is just part of the story. Historically, until the 1970s—going all the way back to the fifteenth century, for as long as there are continuous records—bull markets in gold occurred during periods of *deflation*. In fact, there are no examples of deflationary periods in which gold's purchasing power didn't increase.

This is not as odd or inconsistent as it might seem. Gold's unique qualities, which give it universal credibility as a medium of exchange, propel it to the fore during extreme economic scenarios of any sort. It serves as a rationing mechanism for scarcities of any kind—and this includes debt. This is why gold has been a stellar performer during deflationary periods, including deflationary times that also included economic growth. (While the combination of deflation and strong growth may seem counterintuitive, it has occurred, for example, at times during the latter part of the nineteenth century.) In the 1930s, during the Great Depression, gold was by far the best-performing asset around. So yes, gold is an inflation hedge, but it's a deflation hedge as well.

And just to make sure I've left no loose ends in the inflation/deflation discussion of gold, I want to make crystal clear that in talking about gold's role as an inflation hedge, I am referring solely to inflation as defined by rising commodities. This is what inflation means. It doesn't mean the measure many people have been led to believe represents inflation, the Consumer Price Index (CPI).

During the 1970s' gold bull market, the CPI surged. Prior to that decade, the CPI had rarely topped 5 percent a year. In the 1970s, it rose at an annualized rate of more than 8 percent. In fact, it more than doubled—likely surpassing every other decade in this country's history.

In contrast, in the 2000s' bull market in gold, the CPI gained an average 2.2 percent a year, well *below* historical averages and just around 30 percent of its rate in the 1970s. In other words, one bull market in gold occurred with near-record high rises in the CPI, whereas the other bull market took place when the CPI barely budged.

Moreover, during the 1980s and 1990s, with gold in a generation-long downtrend, the CPI was higher—indeed, considerably higher—than during the 2000s' bull market in gold. If this surprises you, it points to the failings of the CPI as a measure of inflation. The CPI isn't a true measure of inflation at all. Rather, it's a cost-of-living index, and a flawed one at that. I look at it in Chapter 18 so I won't get in the weeds here. The main point I'll make here is that the only meaningful measure of inflation is changes in commodity prices. When it comes to where gold is headed, ignore the CPI and keep your attention firmly fixed on commodity prices.

And commodity prices are headed up as the world, particularly the emerging world led by China, moves to create infrastructure on an unprecedented scale. This effort will mean rising demand for commodities, resulting in the kinds of scarcities that go hand in hand with rising gold.

4

The Coming Infrastructure Explosion: Part 1

I HAVEN'T READ every comment Xi Jinping has made since he became China's president in 2013. But I feel very confident in venturing to say that not once has he referred to, much less tweeted about, "infrastructure week." China and its leaders, as I've said before, are long-term oriented. They don't do weeks.

Instead, China has made, and will be making for years, vast investments in infrastructure both within its own boundaries and, on an even greater scale, throughout the developing world via its Belt and Road Initiative (BRI). China's infrastructure push is something every investor, and particularly every investor interested in gold, should care about a lot. Why? Because it will consume massive amounts of commodities. This will lead to commodity scarcities and rising prices, the conditions that go hand in hand with bull markets in gold.

Infrastructure covers the gamut of fixed physical assets needed to provide for the common good, including those related to supplying power, water, transport, and communications. It includes roads, rails, seaports and airports, cables and water pipes, dams and hydroelectric plants, oil and gas pipelines and terminals, solar panels and wind turbines, and electric grids. It further includes installations needed for the internet and the transmission of digital data, the volume of which is growing by leaps and bounds. The onset of fifth-generation (5G) wireless networks will be the latest digital expansion that will vastly increase the need for infrastructure to accommodate it.

None of these things are conjured out of thin air. They require steel, copper, zinc, silver, and, leading the pack, essential in creating and running everything, energy. The greater the scope of the infrastructure creation that lies ahead, the greater will be the future demand for commodities.

Infrastructure creation is just the start, however. Once built, good infrastructure doesn't just sit there—it promotes economic growth, and that, in turn, leads to further demand for resources. Infrastructure is the great enabler of commerce and growth. An economy can't function if goods can't be shipped from one place to another, if there aren't docks for loading and unloading goods, if energy and water can't flow to factories and homes, if there aren't cities where people can come together and work, if people and companies lack the means to communicate.

The initial building of infrastructure will devour huge amounts of commodities. After that, though, infrastructure generates a further call on resources, especially in developing countries. As infrastructure spurs economic growth and raises living standards, demand will grow for more *things*—cars to drive along those new roads, air conditioners and washing machines for all the buildings going up in new or expanding urban centers, cell phones and TVs, and more. These products, too, require large quantities of commodities. China's push to build infrastructure at home and throughout the developing world is tantamount to a vast acceleration in demand for resources of all kinds.

China, the United States, and Rail

Infrastructure, of course, does get talked about in the United States as well. The need to improve and replace aging infrastructure in this country is clear, and Republicans and Democrats alike agree that it's essential. As indeed it is. How essential? The American Society of Civil Engineers (ASCE) issues report cards every four years evaluating the state of U.S. infrastructure. The latest was in 2017, when the United States got a D+, the same grade it received in 2013. The ASCE estimates the United States would need to spend $4.5 trillion by 2025 to bring infrastructure here up to acceptable levels. And this might understate the need as crisis after crisis erupts, from bridges collapsing to devasting wildfires in California. The 2018 "camp fire" in California, the most destructive in history, involved the snapping of transmission lines that had been installed in 1921.

Despite the obvious and urgent need for a major national commitment to upgrade U.S. infrastructure from sea to shining sea (and actually, what with polluted beaches and oceans, they're not so shining any more), little is being done commensurate with the need. If the United States gets its act together and spends the trillions of dollars needed, this would add to the overall amount of infrastructure creation in coming years and to the demand for commodities. But any efforts by the United States would still be dwarfed by what is going on in the East led by China. As long as China remains on track, the infrastructure explosion will happen.

According to the latest data supplied by the International Monetary Fund (IMF), for the five-year stretch between 2010 and 2015, China spent about 8.3 percent of its gross domestic product (GDP) on infrastructure. This compares to 2.3 percent for the United States and translates into $8 trillion worth of new infrastructure—close to the entire infrastructure base of the United States, which is estimated at around $10 trillion.

The Organisation for Economic Co-operation and Development (OECD) supplies more recent data. The data indicate that in 2017,

China spent around $635 billion on transportation infrastructure, including road, rail, airports, and waterways. The United States spent $90 billion, much of it in the form of repairs rather than adding to the existing base.

Homing in on just one form of infrastructure, rail, conveys a sense of China's ability to act, as opposed to talk, and to act efficiently. In 2007, according to the Asian Development Bank, China had 48,000 total rail miles. Some 15,000 miles were electrified, and 252 miles were high speed. (High-speed rail has to be electrified, but not all electrified track is high speed.)

By 2010, the number had risen to 57,000 total miles, 3,000 of which were high speed. This would mean that by the end of 2020, high-speed rail would make up 10 percent of total rail miles, up from just a fraction of 1 percent in 2007.

The United States has 140,000 miles of rail track. Most of it was built before 1930, and some of it goes back to the 1850s. No new track has been built since 1950. Less than 1 percent of the total is even electrified—only around 1,400 miles. What's the advantage of electrified trains compared with diesel-powered trains? Among other things, they bring faster travel times because trains can accelerate more quickly from station stops. They are cheaper and more reliable, going far longer before needing maintenance. There is less wear and tear on tracks. And trains can run on renewable fuels because solar and wind energy can be turned into electricity and transmitted via an electrical grid. Around the globe, electricity serves nearly a quarter of railroad track miles and supplies more than one-third of the energy that powers trains.

As for high-speed rail, it transports large numbers of people between cities faster and more reliably than cars or planes can do (after accounting for travel time to airports, waiting times to board, delays for bad weather, etc.). Beijing-based journalist Frank Sieren, writing for the German business publication *Handelsblatt*, reported that in late 2017, China's high-speed rail network—eight separate lines running north-south and east-west—accounted for around two-thirds of the global network. By 2030, China aims to have 80 percent of Chinese cities with populations greater than 1 million linked to the network.

One of China's newest high-speed trains, called the Fuxing—meaning "renewal"—began operating in September 2017. It makes the 808-mile trip between Beijing and Shanghai in about four and a half hours. This easily bests Germany's high-speed trains, which take six hours to travel between Hamburg and Munich, around half the distance. According to Sieren, China spent $118 billion on high-speed rail in 2016 and has put aside half a trillion dollars for high-speed rail travel in its current five-year plan. Most recently, in September 2018, China inaugurated a 16-mile high-speed rail link between Hong Kong and the mainland city of Guangzhou, from where it will connect to China's existing high-speed rail network.

As for the United States, consider California's long-time and still-futile effort to create a high-speed rail link between Los Angeles and San Francisco. The effort was approved in a 2008 referendum vote, with a projected budget of $40 billion. It then underwent various reviews and studies. In March 2018, a new draft plan was issued that estimated that the cost would exceed $77 billion and possibly go far higher—and projected the first bullet trains might run by 2027, though not very far.

Rail is just one example of China's rapid and efficient infrastructure buildup at home, albeit the one that's most often cited. Its electric grid is another.

Ultra-High-Voltage Grid

In November 2018, *Nextbigfuture*, a science-oriented web publication, carried an article headlined "China's Giant Ultra-High-Voltage Grid Is as Ambitious as Its High-Speed Rail." Ultra-high-voltage (UHV) power lines transmit energy at ultrarapid speeds, allowing electricity to travel long distances with very little power loss. It means that power generated in one region can travel across continent-wide stretches to run factories, light homes, and so on. As a result, UHV power lines make it possible for the electricity generated by power sources such as hydropower dams, which are often located far away from the densely populated regions where power is most needed, to quickly and efficiently get to where the power can do the most good.

One of China's UHV lines, for instance, brings power 1,680 kilometers from the Xiloudu Dam in the Southwest to Zhejiang province in China's East. It contributed an estimated 17 percent of Zhejiang's power in the summer, replacing more than 30 million tons of coal and cutting air pollution.

In early 2019, *Bloomberg* reported that China's State Grid Corporation had started up the world's largest, most powerful UHV power line. The next month, the Institute of Electrical and Electronics Engineers (IEEE) reported that China had completed 19 of 30 planned lines.

In an article on June 6, 2018, the *Financial Times* cited Stephen Chu, the Nobel prize–winning physicist who served as President Obama's energy secretary, as saying that "China has the best transmission lines in terms of the highest voltage and lowest loss. They can transmit electricity over 2,000 km and lose only 7% of the energy. If we transmitted over 200 km we would lose more than that."

Ghost Cities

Some in the West have looked at some of China's infrastructure efforts with a skeptical eye. You may have heard of China's so-called ghost cities. While the term is meant to be derisive, I happen to like it. Maybe it evokes for me the kinds of eerie, scary stories I used to enjoy reading as a boy or raises fond memories of Rod Serling's *Twilight Zone* (even in this golden age of streaming, one of the all-time greatest TV shows ever made, in my opinion).

However, if China's ghost cities are scary, it should be for another reason. They demonstrate, once again, China's scary-smart willingness to think long term, an attribute that gives China an enormous edge as it pursues its vision of remaking the world order.

Western journalists coined the phrase *ghost cities* back around 2009 to describe (and pan) huge urban areas China was creating, either as stand-alone cities or as adjuncts to existing urban centers. These cities had miles of streets, apartment buildings, office buildings, and schools. The only thing they lacked was people.

Time magazine published a photo essay showing one such ghost city, Ordos, in Inner Mongolia—more than a dozen photos of brand-new but clearly uninhabited buildings and streets. And in March 2013, CBS's *60 Minutes* crew traveled to Zhenghou's Zhengdon New District, reporting back that "[w]e found what they call a 'ghost city' of new towers with no residents, desolate condos and vacant subdivisions uninhabited for miles and miles and miles."

The ghost cities were jeered at as signs of reckless, mindless spending that was sure to end badly. But a few years later, the laugh was on us. Wade Shepard, author of the book, *Ghost Cities of China*, noted in a May 26, 2015, article in the *South China Morning Post* that at least 1.4 million people had moved into Zhengdong New District, with more on the way, ready to take advantage of the "steady increase in public services, transport infrastructure, commercial outlets, educational facilities and employment opportunities" that he said had transformed the district.

> The 150 sq km new area to the east of the city is divided into a central business district (CBD), a university town, a science and technology park, a commercial logistics zone, and an economic and technological development area. All this is in a place where there was nothing but fallow construction land about 12 years ago.

In a later piece in *Forbes*, written in January 2016, Shepard noted how China skillfully uses the creation of universities as a way to pull people into newly created urban centers.

> Often built into the master plans of many of the country's large new areas are massive university towns, where more than

a dozen new campuses can be built side by side that will bring in, literally, hundreds of thousands of students and staff. The idea is that seeding a developing area with a fledgling population base can initiate the beginnings of a local business ecosystem, which will then make the place more attractive to prospective home buyers and residents, which will then attract even more businesses.

The overall point is that the new infrastructure underpins China's unprecedented urbanization program. China has undertaken an ambitious effort to raise the incomes of its rural population by moving some 250 million villagers into newly built towns and cities by 2025, with an urbanization target of 70 percent. A McKinsey study projects that by then China will have more than 220 cities with populations of at least 1 million compared with 125 in 2010.

China has a history of building major real estate developments before residents move in. Pudong, an outgrowth of Shanghai, was also once known as a "ghost town" but is now a thriving financial and commercial hub with more than 5 million residents. The West may think it imprudent to build before demand has fully materialized, but China takes the opposite approach, putting cities in place to meet its ambitious urbanization targets.

The saga of ghost cities exemplifies two consistent realities that bear on the world's future. One is China's ability to carry out long-term plans. The other is the West's consistent misreading of China's actions, with a clear bias toward viewing them in a negative light, a tendency that emerges time and again in many different contexts. Both these realities are not helpful to the West, but they are good news for gold.

Some Big Numbers

Various organizations have assessed global infrastructure needs, and they all project that infrastructure spending will need to rise sharply for decades, from the current level of under $3 trillion a year to as much as $9 trillion a year. Whichever figure comes closest to the bull's eye, they all imply enormous demand for resources for a long time to come. In today's world, it's easy to be distracted by day-to-day crises and controversies. It's important not to lose sight of some of the longer-term trends that ultimately may have the biggest impact on your life and finances. The coming infrastructure explosion, with its implications for gold, is one of the most important of those trends.

China's efforts within its own borders are one part of it and show what the country is capable of doing. But it's the huge infrastructure investments China is making throughout the rest of the developing world through its ambitious BRI that will be truly transformative.

5

The Coming Infrastructure Explosion, Part 2

GRANTED, BY THE standards of Western tabloids, it wasn't the catchiest headline around. But it did make the point. On September 7, 2013, China's ministry of foreign affairs issued a statement about an address delivered at Kazakhstan's Nazarbayev University headlined, "President Xi Delivers Important Speech and Proposes to Build a Silk Economic Belt with Central Asian Countries."

An important speech indeed—the first public iteration of Xi's ambitious, expansive plan to link, by land and sea, economies of Central Asia and South Asia with China and each other and with lands beyond. Evoking the old Silk Road traveled by Marco Polo in the thirteenth century, the initial plan had two parts: a land route called the *Silk Road Economic Belt* and a waterway route called the *21st Century Maritime Silk Road*. Together they made up what Xi first called China's

One Belt One Road initiative, a term later replaced by Belt and Road Initiative (BRI).

Whatever the name, it was a giant undertaking that got underway quickly and has expanded rapidly ever since.

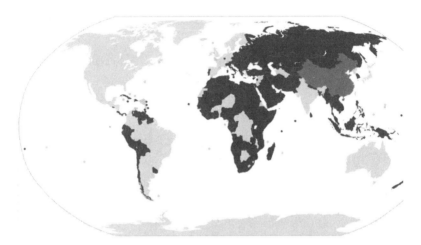

FIGURE 5.1   Countries participating in Belt and Road Initiative as of April 2019
Source: Wikipedia

Within fairly short order, the project extended to more than 65 countries with a combined gross domestic product (GDP) of at least $23 trillion and populations totaling 4.4 billion people—roughly 62 percent of the world's population and 30 percent of global economic output. By 2019, according to *Nature* magazine, BRI had activities in or arrangements with some 120 partner countries in all corners of the globe. It is estimated that China eventually will invest between $1 trillion and $8 trillion in BRI projects.

The initiative reaches into the Arctic in a so-called Polar Silk Road and extends into Eastern European countries. It encompasses projects in South America, including in Brazil, where China is installing an ultra-high-voltage power line using the technology and expertise applied in the lines it has installed domestically.

In 2019, Italy became the first major Western European country to participate in BRI as it welcomed a commitment by China to upgrade three Italian ports. Later in the year, the small German city of Arnstadt welcomed the overtures of a Chinese company, CATL, to invest more than $2 billion to build, in an adjoining industrial park, a factory that will produce batteries for electric cars.

BRI has been called the largest development project in modern history. Initially, it was compared with the Marshall Plan, but its scope has grown far larger as it has burgeoned. The initiative accounts for a large chunk of the coming infrastructure explosion that lies ahead. It truly is an example of China thinking long term—of having "the vision thing" (to use the phrase made famous by a frustrated Vice President George H. W. Bush in 1988 as he notably failed to offer any such inspiration during that year's presidential campaign). This vision begins with China as the hub of a vast Eastern trading region connected and made prosperous with the help of China-funded infrastructure and energy investments and willing to let China set the rules of the road. Beyond its economic goals, it also has clear geopolitical ramifications, further elevating China's position as a world power.

I wasn't inside Xi's head when he first began thinking about and refining ideas for BRI, which follows and builds on but vastly enlarges the scope of earlier Chinese moves to forge ties with developing countries. But I could imagine him looking one evening at a map of the world and saying to himself, "Wow, look at all these sleepy (and resource-rich) countries right in our neighborhood. Turkmenistan. Kazakhstan. Uzbekistan. Kyrgyzstan. Not all that much going on there—I've heard they hardly trade among themselves at all—what a waste—and what an opportunity. Let's put some money in them, help them build roads and rail terminals or something, and factories, and pipelines, and get something going. That will get economic activity there humming, which will bring in further investment, and wouldn't that be nice for them, and for us, too, because who are they going to trade with if not with us. And let's focus on transportation projects—make it easier for people and goods to travel from the Pacific to the Baltic Sea. Connectivity—that's the ticket—that's the word to stress. Lots of energy projects, too—can't run an economy without reliable energy. This could be big!"

I can imagine him growing even more enthusiastic as he envisioned additional possibilities. Perhaps he told himself, "I really am a genius, because why stop with Central Asia. We can take these regional links farther, extending them all the way to the developed countries of Europe—which, trust me, are going be dying to be part of this thing once they realize its potential, how many millions of people in the East will have more money to spend. . . . And come to think of it, this could be a helluva good way to deal with China's excess manufacturing capacity, bailing out all our factories that helped propel China's breakneck growth this century but that now are producing more steel and cement than we know what to do with here. What a perfect solution—just shift them somewhere else, where they're needed—keeping our economy growing at the same time!

"And of course, if it turns out some of those countries have strategic value to us—never hurts to have a port in India's neighborhood is what I say!—so much the better. Not to mention that by linking China's pesky western provinces more closely to Pakistan, it will facilitate their development and might take some pressure off me on that front. . . .

"Speaking of Pakistan—and that deep water port, Gwadar—if we build it up, it sure will make shipping oil from the Middle East to China a lot faster and cheaper. I'll have to check the numbers tomorrow, too tired to get up and do it now, but rough back-of-the-envelope guesstimate, it should cut the miles in half, that's not chopped liver, whatever the heck that means—and it would solve our Malacca dilemma [here Xi is musing about the fact that around 85 percent of China's oil imports travel through a narrow chokepoint of the Strait of Malacca, leaving China vulnerable in the event it ever were cut off]."

And finally, as he was drifting off, he might have muttered to himself, "Mustn't forget about soft power—if we're the ones building infrastructure, we're the ones who can set the technical standards for rail and other industries—a very important advantage to us and our industries. Make note in the morning."

Well, maybe this is not exactly how BRI came into being. It does, though, give some sense of what the initiative represents both for China and for the world. Xi himself, at a forum in May 2017 for heads of state of countries participating in BRI, expressed the initiative's basic purpose more prosaically and succinctly, saying: "In pursuing the Belt and Road Initiative, we should focus on the fundamental issue of development, release the growth potential of various countries and achieve economic integration and interconnected development and deliver benefits to all."

The U.S. View

When Xi first announced the initiative in 2013, it didn't get much attention in the Western press. Now, more than half a decade past BRI's launch, the West has definitely sat up and taken notice—usually in a negative way, with almost every article that mentions BRI containing an almost obligatory boilerplate sentence exuding skepticism about the initiative's goals and implementation.

You could easily assume two rather contradictory things. One is that BRI really isn't going all that well—that it's running into pushback from the countries China is wooing and could fizzle out. Second, and suggesting quite the opposite conclusion—that BRI is proceeding all too well—is that it represents a threat to Western interests and dominance that the West must resist.

A common theme is that in investing huge sums in infrastructure projects, China essentially has played a trick on the countries it is purportedly helping. One frequent assertion is that China's loans come with onerous terms that leave participating countries helplessly flailing in a debt trap, in some cases forcing them to cede vital interests to China. Other raps are that the infrastructure projects being funded are poorly conceived, or damaging to the environment, or are carried out by Chinese workers rather than employing local residents.

The United States has tried to steer potential BRI recipient countries away from China's embrace. Vice President Pence, addressing

Asian leaders at the Asia Pacific Economic Cooperation (APEC) forum in late 2018, called BRI a "constricting belt" and "one-way road." Similarly, in 2019 testimony before the Senate's Armed Services Committee, General Joseph Dunford, head of the U.S. Joint Chiefs of Staff, slammed China for its "predatory economics" designed to expand its global influence.

Most BRI countries themselves don't seem persuaded by this view. But let's grant for a moment that the skeptics have a point. Let's agree that you can question China's motives and lending terms. Let's concur that China should be more environmentally conscious in its projects (and, actually, according to a recent study by *Nature* magazine, it has become increasingly attentive to environmental issues and the concerns of the populations of BRI participant countries). Let's posit anything you want.

The point is that focusing on those concerns, whether they're legitimate or not, is a bit like having an elephant saunter into your living room and you getting all worked up because it has mud on its feet that it's tracking into the house. Yes, it certainly would have been preferable if the elephant had considerately wiped its feet before entering. But you have an elephant in your living room that shows no signs of leaving anytime soon, if ever. It's taking up a lot of space and changing the calculus of how you can use your house. And really, the mud is the least of your concerns.

For investors, the key takeaway from BRI should be that it is fostering infrastructure creation on an enormous scale. In itself, the infrastructure creation ensures demand for commodities. Even more to the point, improved infrastructure will propel economic growth throughout the developing world, keeping demand for commodities humming long after the roads and rails and air terminals and energy pipelines have been completed. Whatever your ideology or politics, this is the reality. And it all points to higher gold prices.

The China–Pakistan Economic Corridor and Connectivity

BRI is big, multifaceted, and continually evolving, an enormous global grab bag of projects financed through generally low-interest loans by an array of Chinese companies. But some of the projects are more significant than others, directly transforming global trade networks.

The biggest BRI undertaking is the China–Pakistan Economic Corridor (CPEC). It stretches 3,000 kilometers from Kashgar in China's far western province of Xinjiang to Pakistan's deepwater port of Gwadar on the Arabian Sea.

Formalized in April 2015, CPEC initially encompassed 51 separate agreements and additional memorandums of understanding specifying highways, railways, and energy installations along the corridor. Energy and transportation projects make up the lion's share of the projects.

China planned at first to invest $46 billion in CPEC over a 10- to 15-year period. This figure has since been raised to at least $62 billion. By way of comparison, the original $46 billion was more than double all foreign direct investment in Pakistan since 2008.

A key component of CPEC was enlargement of Gwadar, which is near the Persian Gulf. Pakistan has leased the port through 2059 to the state-owned Chinese Overseas Ports Holding Company. A special economic zone (SEZ) next to the port—one of at least seven SEZs planned as part of CPEC—is due for completion by the end of 2020.

The importance to Pakistan of China's investments was highlighted in a lengthy paper presented at the April 2018 CPEC summit held in Pakistan. Its author was Ahsan Iqbal, who at the time was Pakistan's federal minister for planning, development, and reform. The key to CPEC, Iqbal said, was the connectivity China was providing. "This is the basic essence of BRI: this huge network of corridors. Connectivity is going to bring new demand and growth in the world economy."

Since then, it's no secret that Pakistan's economy has soured. Growth has declined, and foreign reserves have been sharply drawn down, threatening Pakistan's ability to meet debt obligations, including billions owed to China. Some commentators have argued that CPEC deserves some of the blame by increasing Pakistan's debt load, sometimes to fund projects that were poorly conceived in the first place. And any further progress in CPEC, they say, is likely to be limited.

But the Voice of America has reported that following completion of its first 22 projects, CPEC has entered its next stage. It will include an international airport in Gwadar and creation of nine industrial zones. These eventually should improve Pakistan's foreign reserves posture by boosting Pakistani exports. And in April 2019, at the second BRI forum, China and Pakistan signed agreements for a host of additional projects, including upgrading a Karachi–Peshawar railway line.

BRI's Impact on Growth

A recent study by Moody's Analytics helps illuminate both why BRI will add so significantly to global growth and why the debt burden on participants is less problematic than often painted. The study described the strong links between improved infrastructure, increased trade, and stronger growth. It highlighted an estimate by the World Bank that infrastructure improvements in BRI countries will increase trade among them by as much as 4.1 percent a year.

The study noted, too, that many BRI countries have low debt ratings, making them hard pressed to attract investors or obtain loans without committing to making a lot of reforms. Thus, until now, their economies have gone nowhere. China, with its willingness to invest in them without imposing any conditions, is bringing them into the global economic fold, adding to the totality of countries contributing to global economic activity.

The study also noted that while loans from China increase debt in absolute terms, debt as a percentage of GDP starts to shrink once infrastructure is in place and begins to generate growth.

Finally, the study notes that setbacks widely publicized in the West as demonstrating that BRI's appeal is fading have often proved temporary. For instance, in 2018, after a new government was voted into office, Malaysia suspended construction of the East Coast Rail Link, a 398-mile rail line being built with a Chinese loan. The new president of Malaysia had campaigned against the project, arguing that the terms were onerous.

But China was willing to renegotiate the terms, and a year later, construction resumed. Malaysia's finance minister has said that the country is now considering additional investments with China, which is Malaysia's largest trading partner.

At the second BRI forum, in April 2019, President Xi addressed many of the criticisms of BRI, saying that China would make the process of awarding contracts more open and competitive and would be more attentive to environmental concerns. You may or may not take these promises at face value. I take them as showing that China is continuing to play the long game and will adjust its tactics as it proceeds to where it knows it is going.

The bottom line is that BRI is for real and that it's big. It's not a blip or a passing fancy. You can't ignore its impact just because you don't like all that China is doing. It will continue to expand and to accelerate growth in developing economies.

And this is truly consequential. The developing world has become more significant to global growth than the developed world, giving it unprecedented influence over what happens everywhere, including in your own portfolios. You can draw a clear line between growth in the developing world and a bull market in gold.

6
Not the Same Old Developing World

TOM STOPPARD'S PLAY, *Rosencrantz and Guildenstern Are Dead*, first produced in 1967, is based on the conceit of taking two minor characters from *Hamlet* and making them the main players. That premise isn't a bad way to understand the breakout role the developing world is seizing today vis-à-vis the developed world.

Developing countries used to be bit players in the global economy. They contributed to the overall action largely as suppliers of essential commodities to the marquee countries like the United States that played leading roles. But individually and as a collection, their economies were too small to have much of an impact on the world as a whole.

When Western economies were thriving, world growth was strong, and demand for commodities would rise, benefiting developing countries. When Western economies faltered, during the Depression or various recessions, demand for commodities would drop.

But today those dynamics are shifting in a big and very consequential way. Through the Belt and Road Initiative (BRI) and various trade agreements, China is unleashing the growth potential of developing countries and making it possible for them to surmount obstacles that held them back in the past. Increasingly, in contrast to the past, developing countries are in a position to drive the action when it comes to demand for commodities.

To put it another way, this isn't the same old developing world that you may remember and most likely didn't pay much attention to. Understanding how the developing world is different—different from what it used to be and different from the United States and the West—is another important part of understanding the case for gold.

The first thing to know about how the developing world is different today is that in toto and when measured by the most meaningful yardstick—known as *purchasing power parity* (PPP)—it is now bigger in economic size than the developed world. This major inflection point occurred in 2011. The next thing to realize is that the developing world is growing faster than the developed world. This means that the gap between the two will continue to widen.

These two facts, in tandem, say that something brand new is happening in the world. For the first time ever, the biggest part of the world is also the fastest growing. The implications are enormous.

Economic growth goes hand in hand with demand for commodities. When the biggest chunk of the world is also the fastest growing, it portends accelerated demand for resources of all kinds. This is particularly true because growth in developing economies is more commodity intensive than growth in developed economies, which are more dependent on their service sectors.

If this sounds somewhat abstract, an analogy may help. Imagine that you own two dogs: an eight-week-old Saint Bernard puppy that weighs 25 pounds and an adult golden retriever that has topped out at 75 pounds. Initially, it costs more to feed your goldie, which consumes around 3½ cups or so of kibble each day compared with around 1½ cups for the new puppy. But your puppy is growing rapidly, putting on weight at the rate of three or more pounds a week and requiring more kibble all the time. By the time the puppy reaches 75 pounds, it will still only be 12 months old, with two more years of growth ahead, and it has begun to consume more kibble than your goldie by an ever-expanding amount.

When it comes to demand for kibble, now it's the giant newcomer that has the greatest impact on your pet food budget. You can only hope that kibble—unlike most commodities—won't be experiencing scarcities anytime soon.

Size Matters

Comparing the relative sizes of two dogs is easy: you simply put them on a scale. Comparing the relative sizes of economies, though, can be more controversial. You still hear all the time that China is the world's second-biggest economy, after the United States. This is true when you measure each country's size in dollars, as is typically done. But, as I indicated earlier, there's a more relevant yardstick: PPP. Using this measure, China already is the world's largest economy. And similarly, in economic size, the developing world as a whole, including China, overshadows the developed world.

In case you think that in using PPP as a measure of size I am somehow cheating, trying to sneak in some nefarious sleight of hand, here's a quick explanation of what PPP is and why it's an appropriate way to compare economies.

Under the more traditional approach, all economic activity in a country is expressed in dollar terms, and economies are compared with one another based on the dollar amounts of all their transactions. For the United States, this is straightforward. You simply add up all economic activity in a year—manufacturing output, sales, services, and so on—to arrive at gross domestic product (GDP). That's all you have to do because all these items are already expressed in dollar amounts.

For all other countries, which have their own currencies, there's an added step. Economic activity is reported in the local currency, which then must be translated into a dollar figure based on the prevailing currency exchange rates. Then you can proceed with comparisons expressed in dollars.

Although this might seem like a fair enough approach, it can be misleading, giving a false impression of how big one economy is compared with another. That's because it doesn't necessarily tell you anything about the volume of goods and services within a country, which, in the final analysis, is what really matters. This is where PPP comes in. It takes into account the cost of living in a particular country and approaches the question of relative size by looking at how much of a similar basket of goods people in one country can buy compared with people in other countries for the same number of dollars.

If you've heard of *The Economist*'s famous annual "Big Mac" survey, then you've already encountered the concept of PPP. *The Economist* employs it as a way to assess whether a country's currency is under- or overvalued. The survey assumes that Big Mac hamburgers are the same all around the globe (though that's not quite true; McDonald's varies ingredients to appeal to local tastes). It then compares prices in different countries.

On a random day in 2019, a Big Mac was going for €3.85 in Italy, which translated into $4.23. That same day, Americans (in some cities, at least) were paying $5.30. You can conclude that the euro was undervalued relative to the dollar.

This is one way to make use of the concept of PPP. But it also comes into play in comparing the true size, as opposed to the dollar size, of different economies.

A commonsense way to understand this distinction is to think about the real estate market. Clearly, if you are looking to own a house, a buck goes a lot further in some places than in others.

For instance, a four-bedroom house on two acres of land in an upscale suburb in New York's Westchester County might go for $2.5 million. The exact same house, identical in size and decor down to the last bathroom tile, and also sited on two acres of land would certainly go for a lot less in, say, Indiana. I've never house hunted in Indiana (nor do I live in Westchester), but let's posit that in Indiana, the same house would cost only $500,000.

Thus, if you had a community in New York with 10 such houses at $2.5 million each and a community in Indiana also with 10 such houses, and taking only this real estate into account, the New York community would have a value of $25 million versus $5 million for the Indiana locale.

Let's take it a step further. Suppose that Westchester County still has those 10 houses. But in Indiana, there aren't just 10 houses, there are 30! Indiana wins hands down when it comes to actual house wealth. It has far more bedrooms, far more bathrooms, far more kitchens. But still, at $500,000 per house, in dollar terms, Indiana's real estate comes to only $15 million. It still lags New York despite its greater wealth in houses.

A final thought: each of Indiana's houses requires the same amounts of resources to be built as the houses in New York (remember, all the houses are identical), but because there are more of them, they will consume more resources in toto. And houses, as any homeowner knows, are bottomless money pits—each house will continue to consume energy and from time to time require paint, new windows and roofs, not to mention all the daily supplies from toilet paper to laundry detergent—with, again, greater demand in aggregate coming from the nominally poorer Indiana township.

Applying this analogy to the world today, the bottom line is that the discrepancies in economic size between low- and high-income countries can be a lot smaller than would appear simply by comparing their dollar GDP. It can even be that a lower-income country has a bigger economy overall.

This is the case with China today vis-à-vis the United States. Every three years, the World Bank releases a report comparing the world's economies in terms of PPP and U.S. dollars. The most recent report was in 2017. It showed that calculated in PPP, China's economy is 21 percent larger than the U.S. economy and 11 percent larger than that of the European Union.

And led by China, the economy of the developing world as a whole, as I noted earlier, is larger than that of the developed world. Today the developed world, with just around 20 percent of the world's population, accounts for roughly 45 percent of global GDP. Its share of the global economy will shrink further as developing countries continue to outgrow the developed world.

Defining the Developing World

Before continuing with my look at the developing world, I should stop to define it. I've used the term dozens of times already, but what exactly is the developing world? It's not as simple a question as you might think.

In fact, in 2016, the World Bank, whose mandate is to help fund development in less developed countries, decided that it no longer would use the term *developing world* at all, feeling that it was outdated (similar to how *third world*, the term used during cold war days, eventually became passé). Instead, the World Bank now simply classifies all countries into four income groups based on gross per-capita income. The income levels that define the categories change somewhat from year to year depending on inflation and other considerations. For fiscal year 2018, the World Bank defined low-income countries as those with per-capita incomes of $1,005 or less; lower-middle-income countries, $1,006–$3,955; upper-middle-income countries, $3,956–$12,235; and high-income countries, $12,236 and above.

But this is just one of various approaches used to slice and dice countries and regions according to their relative economic status. The United Nations, for instance, doesn't stop with income levels but applies other criteria to declare that some countries are simultaneously high income *and* developing. Examples include the six Mideastern countries in the Gulf Cooperation Council: Saudi Arabia, Kuwait, the United Arab Emirates, Qatar, Bahrain, and Oman. All are classified as developing. This is quite striking when you consider that in 2015, Qatar's per-capita income was $124,740—more than double the 2016 level of $58,030 in the United States.

On a more philosophical plane, moreover, if you take literally the definition of a developed country offered by former UN Secretary General Kofi Annan, I'd argue that no country, including the United

States, could accurately be called developed. Annan defines a developed country as "one that allows all its citizens to enjoy a free and healthy life in a safe environment." By this standard, I can't think of a single country that qualifies.

For the purposes of my own analysis, I've decided that for convenience's sake, I'll be old school and continue to use the terms *developed* and *developing*. In using the former term, I'm referring to countries with per-capita incomes of $12,236 or higher. The latter term refers to everyone else. It's a serviceable distinction that works well in analyzing the data and that captures the key dichotomy that will increasingly shape the global economy.

The Importance of Connectivity

The developing world isn't changing just by becoming bigger relative to the developed world. It also is changing by becoming—thanks largely to China—more connected than ever before. The importance of connectivity was highlighted in the passage I cited in Chapter 5 from the address by former Pakistani Minister Ahsan Iqbal. It applies not just to Pakistan but also to the developing world at large.

With the BRI and other ventures, China is doing more than building physical structures within individual developing countries. It's also forging new linkages—both physical and relational—*among* developing countries. These interconnections vastly leverage the growth potential of each individual country and enhance the overall sway of the developing world as a whole.

Infrastructure itself facilitates such linkages by providing the physical basis for trade and travel among countries. China is further bolstering such ties through a slew of trade and security relationships and investment vehicles.

In the past, poorer countries also sought to develop, to become richer and raise living standards. They relied largely on the World Bank to provide loans and assistance while also trying to attract private investment. But it was a tough slog, with a lot of external and self-created obstacles.

The developing world encompasses a large assortment of countries in various stages of development operating under a variety of political structures. For most of their histories since freeing themselves of colonial masters, developing countries have been relatively isolated, sputtering along on their own, lacking direction, and easily thrown off course. Development proceeded in a scattershot manner from country to country.

Many of the same problems that have long afflicted many of these countries, such as corruption and political instability, still exist. But now countervailing positive forces are emerging as developing countries join in a common search for strong and sustained economic growth. Connectivity is helping to unleash the enormous inherent growth potential of emerging economies as China links countries together in trade and security arrangements that benefit them all.

One example is the Shanghai Cooperation Organization (SCO). Launched by China in the mid-1990s, the SCO is a somewhat motley group now encompassing China, Russia, India, Pakistan, and several resource-rich Central Asian countries. The group's mandate is to function as a collection of countries with shared economic incentives and programs as well as shared security platforms.

Particularly notable is that China succeeded in including Pakistan, India, and itself in a single group of countries with multiple shared concerns. Given the bitter historical and ongoing conflicts between Pakistan and India, this is an extraordinary political and economic achievement that speaks volumes about the potential for continued growth in the East and among developing countries.

Stages of Growth

It's true, as described earlier, that the developing world has overtaken the developed world in aggregate economic size. From another perspective, though—per-capita income—the developing world is still much smaller than developed economies. After all, per-capita income is the very definition of a developing economy. This duality, that the developing world is simultaneously big and small, is at the heart of why the developing world has become so important to the global growth, to future demand for commodities, and—I might as well throw it in again, just to remind you of why I'm delving into all this—to gold.

Although the developing world has made enormous strides, it has a lot further to go to approach the living standards of developed countries. At the beginning of this century, average per-capita GDP in the developed world was roughly eight times that of the developing world. Today it is down to five times. This is a big drop but still leaves a large gap to try to make up.

Once per-capita income exceeds $10,000, demand for commodities tends to slow (and demand for some commodities, copper in particular, may actually decline). Today, more than 80 percent of the world's population has per-capita incomes below $10,000. This leaves tremendous room for commodity demand to continue to rise. While it will be growing as fast as it can to catch up, the developing world still has years to go to get close to doing so. This is a strong reason to think that we're many years away from where demand for commodities in the developing world will naturally start to slow.

There's another relevant consideration. Growth in developing economies isn't just faster—it's qualitatively different. Economists describe economies as going through three distinct phases as they move from less to more developed. Primary economies focus on the extraction of resources, whether this means growing food, mining metals, or drilling for oil. Secondary economies have moved up the development ladder to focus on industrial output, using many of the resources they extract to produce finished goods. Economies in this stage of development have a heavy need for resources.

Tertiary economies such as the United States emphasize the service sector, which facilitates the exchange and use of goods. In the U.S. economy, the service sector accounts for close to 80 percent of GDP. It's not until an economy reaches this final phase that you can expect demand for resources to slow down. The developing world is nowhere near the tertiary stage.

If the developing world is now growing faster than the developed world, as it is, it's a change that can be seen putting a logical relationship into place. It's a truism that it's easier to grow faster when you start from a smaller base. Small-capitalization (small-cap) companies, for instance, while riskier, have more growth potential than large-cap companies.

In other words, it was actually going against the natural order of things that until recently the developed world, with its far higher levels of per-capita income, grew as fast as developing economies. What accounted for this was the developed world's greater political stability. (For a crystal-clear understanding of the connection between political stability and a strong economy, I refer you to Venezuela.)

The emergence of China with its commitment to investing in the developing world has put the logical relationship between growth and size firmly in place. Using data based on constant PPP, though any measure of economic performance would show similar results, between 1990 and 2001, the developing and developed worlds marched more or less in lockstep, growing at roughly the same pace. Since 2001, however, when China entered the World Trade Organization, the developing world has left the developed world in the dust. Poorer countries have grown faster in every four-year period. Over the entire period, their growth has been three times as fast, leading up to the watershed year of 2011, when developing economies for the first time accounted for more than 50 percent of global GDP on a PPP basis.

Today, developing countries, which have the most room for growth, actually are growing the fastest. And for the first time, they also constitute the biggest part of the world's economy. Put these two realities together and you have something brand new, with enormous implications for sustained commodity demand and scarcities.

The developing world in the aggregate is the biggest economic force on the planet, barreling along on a growth path that is largely independent of the developed world. China is intent on bringing its own citizens closer to Western standards of living and to take much of the developing world along with it. This goal has implications for commodities that the West today seems to be unaware of or indifferent to. It's a compelling reason to expect gold to soar.

7
Complex Commodities

THE PRECEDING TWO chapters have begun filling in the big picture. China is knitting together the developing world, infrastructure creation will burgeon, and the developing world will become a far more potent force than ever before. But these trends wouldn't matter to the outlook for gold except for one thing—the relentless demand for commodities that they signal.

After all, if the world had endless amounts of easily obtainable commodities of all sorts, developing countries could take all they want, and there still would be plenty to go around. Commodity prices wouldn't rise, and I probably wouldn't be writing this book.

If only. The sad truth is that commodities are not limitless. Or, to be more precise, there are practical limits to how much of them we can obtain, which is far less than what exists in the ground. Obtaining resources already has become more difficult and more costly. But this hasn't gotten the attention it merits.

A lot of people, in fact, dispute the idea that critical scarcities will emerge within any foreseeable time frame. They offer various rationales for why we don't need to worry. One argument is that as commodity prices rise, we'll always be able to find and develop additional sources that will be newly economical for producers to exploit. Therefore, if scarcities emerge, they will be essentially self-correcting, with supply catching up with rising demand as producers find it economically feasible to go after more difficult-to-mine bodies of ore, those that are less accessible or of poorer quality.

This relates to a distinction between reserves and resources. *Resources* refer to ore that's in the ground but that would be money losing to extract under existing prices. *Reserves* refer to the ore that it makes economic sense to mine. When prices for a commodity go up, a portion of a mining company's resources shifts over into the reserves column.

Some people even envision that someday we will solve any problems of resource shortages by turning to outer space. Suppose that the world desperately needs, say, silver for use in solar panels, and it is discovered that the moon contained oodles of silver just below its surface (hence the song "By the Light of the Silvery Moon"). If silver prices rise high enough, say to $5 billion an ounce, wouldn't you expect that some entrepreneur would get very busy ferrying miners to and from the moon? Problem solved.

Resources for most commodities are vast. But assuming that any commodity scarcities that emerge will self-correct as prices rise misses some inconvenient truths.

Head-Spinning Complexity

One such inconvenient truth is that commodities are intricately interlinked in head-spinningly complex ways. To extract one commodity, you need to harness others. As a result, commodity prices tend to be interrelated: when the price for one commodity rises, putatively incentivizing producers to go after it, the prices of other commodities will rise as well, raising producers' costs. It's the proverbial dog chasing its tail: the faster the dog spins around in pursuit, the faster the tail spins out of reach.

Iron ore is found in large amounts around the world, so you might think that scarcities would never be an issue. However, extracting iron ore requires oil, which also is needed to transport the ore to smelters, heat it, and so on. If oil prices are rising, this raises costs at every stage of the process, pushing up the price of steel.

In addition, keep in mind that it takes steel to make the drilling equipment to obtain oil. Moreover, making steel requires other interdependent resources as well. For instance, commodities such as zinc are needed to harden the steel. Obtaining zinc, however, requires energy, which requires steel, which requires oil, which . . .

This is what I mean by head-spinning complexity.

Oil for now is first among equals when it comes to influencing commodity scarcities. Oil prices affect the entire universe of commodities because no matter what commodity you're talking about—including oil itself—it takes energy to get it out of the ground. For a while longer, that energy will come mainly from oil.

Someday, to be sure, assuming that the world is to survive in any recognizable fashion that supports the human race, we will move past oil and rely solely on renewable energies. All the renewable-energy infrastructure necessary for that momentous and essential transition will be built and in place. But we're still decades from that point of total liberation from fossil fuels. Meanwhile, the world will need a lot of oil to create the huge amounts of renewable-energy infrastructure required to get there.

Other factors shed further light on why it's no simple matter to avert resource scarcities. One is that increasingly producers must contend with resource bodies that are more challenging and costly to mine. They are geographically more remote or deeper below the ground or oceans or of inferior grades, meaning that the same amount of ore yields less of the commodity. These factors all make mining increasingly costly both in money and in the energy needed to carry it out.

This should make intuitive sense. The metaphor *low-hanging fruit* may be overused, but it's apt. If you go apple picking at the start of the season, it takes very little effort to quickly fill a basket with fruit plucked from the apple-laden low-hanging branches of a single tree. Later in the season, you may need to scramble up and down a ladder you shift from tree to tree to accomplish the same result, expending a lot more energy in the process.

In some cases, a scarcity in one essential resource may make it actually impossible to fully exploit other essential commodities that might appear to be plentiful. For instance, obtaining resources nearly always requires water—sometimes lots of it. Chile offers a good example of a country superrich in resources, some of which might never see the light of day because there isn't enough water available to extract them while also meeting human needs for water.

Couldn't the problem be solved simply by shipping water in from a country with water to spare, like Canada? Again, you run head on into all the energy it would take to drive the boats that bring the water down, not to mention the energy needed to make the steel to make those boats.

Commodity scarcities loom in unsuspected places. Water scarcities have gotten some attention. But scarcities of sand? In his book, *The World in a Grain of Sand* (Riverhead Books, 2018), Vince Beiser makes a compelling case that the world will be running low on sand. And if you think that this is of concern only to beachgoers, not so. Sand is a critical ingredient in concrete, asphalt, and glass, and it is also used in drilling for oil, especially in obtaining oil from fracking, where it's already in short supply.

Rising per-capita incomes in the developing world will propel demand for sand for homes and buildings. According to Beiser, "by 2030 the world will need to add 4,000 . . . housing units every hour to meet the demand."

Vietnam, one of the world's fastest-growing developing countries, warned in 2017 that its sand would run out within 15 years. Here in the United States, California's Department of Conservation projects that the state has only enough sand to meet one-third of its long-term needs and must start conserving. Again, while sand can be brought in from other places, doing so requires using ever-more amounts of other resources.

It's remarkable to me how little attention has been paid to the significance of the interdependencies among commodities. Instead, the focus has been on one resource at a time—looking for ways to drill oil more efficiently, for instance. But this seems to be a case of missing the forest for the trees.

There is a cluster of resources—including oil—where if any one of them becomes unaffordable to produce, all progress will come to a halt. By *unaffordable*, I mean that to produce the resource will require using more of that same resource than the process yields. If it turns out, for example, that to produce one barrel of oil you use up more than one barrel, it's game over. Ditto for other critical minerals. In my 2009 book, *Game Over* (Hatchette's Business Plus), I explored in detail the significance of the interdependencies among commodities and their potential to derail all progress.

Interrelationships among commodities will become increasingly evident as global development picks up pace. To think that commodity scarcities will be self-correcting is to fundamentally misunderstand how scarcities become self-reinforcing.

Considering Copper

Copper provides a convenient lens through which to understand forthcoming commodity scarcities. The world's most widely used base metal, copper is found everywhere you look, thanks to its superior qualities as a conductor of electricity and heat. It's in our homes' wiring, in our cars and cell phones and television sets, in heating and cooling systems, and in the electric grid. If you happen to live somewhere with a view of the Statue of Liberty, you're gazing at a whole lot of the metal: the iconic beacon is made entirely of copper, some 179,000 pounds of it. It's hard to imagine that the industrial age or the green revolution could have occurred without the broad-based use of copper. Only silver, which is far more expensive, has superior conductivity qualities. Copper also erodes slowly, making it desirable in roofs, gutters, and plumbing.

In other words, copper is part and parcel of just about everything needed for a decent standard of living today, ensuring a steep rise in demand as emerging economies push to catch up. Copper also is essential to reducing carbon emissions. It's a key component of electric vehicles (EVs) and is used in other green energies as well.

How likely is it that copper supply will meet demand in coming years? I'll start with the demand part of the equation. One insight comes from considering China in relation to the rest of the developing world. China's population is huge—around 1.4 billion. In aggregate, though, the rest of the developing world is far bigger—a combined population that is four times China's.

As China urbanized and built infrastructure over the past two decades, its use of copper skyrocketed. Between the end of 2001—when China joined the World Trade Organization—and 2017, global demand for copper grew by around 10 million metric tons. (A metric ton is 1,000 kilograms, which is equivalent to 2,204.6 pounds. Thus it's somewhat larger than the ton as measured in the United States, which is 2,000 pounds.) This entire increase in demand came from China. Quite remarkably, this increase in demand in a little over one decade and a half roughly matched the entire increase in global copper consumption between 1900 and 1995.

Based on these figures, you could make a case that for the rest of the developing world simply to catch up with China—never mind with the developed world—it would raise global demand for copper by 40 million metric tons over approximately the next decade and a half. Meanwhile, China's use of copper will continue to increase as the country builds new megacities and other forms of infrastructure at home. And to all this you have to add whatever increases in demand come from the developed world.

Copper, Cars, and Renewable Energies

Another window into future copper demand comes from looking at copper's use in vehicles, especially in EVs. There are around 1.1 billion cars in existence today. As the developing world increases its living standards, the global car population could easily double or triple or more. Already this century, car sales have been in a striking uptrend. According to Statista, the German online statistics portal, in the 15 years between 2000 and 2015, 54.9 million cars were sold globally. This compares with 77.3 million in 2016 and 79 million in 2017. For 2018, estimated sales were 78.7 million, the same as projected for 2019.

Copper is used in the electronics and wiring of all cars, and rising car sales are guaranteed to boost copper demand. But particularly significant is that a rising proportion of new sales will be EVs. And while all cars require copper, EVs use a lot more.

According to the International Copper Association, while conventional gasoline-powered cars use between 18 and 49 pounds of copper, hybrid electric vehicles contain approximately 85 pounds, plug-in hybrid EVs require 132 pounds, and battery EVs need 183 pounds. More than a mile of copper wiring can be found in an EV's stator winding, the wire coil found in the motor.

Copper is also used in the charging stations where EVs recharge, millions more of which will be needed as EVs gain in popularity. By some estimates, once you take all the infrastructure into account, each EV will use roughly 10 times as much copper as a gasoline-powered vehicle.

China, which is the largest market for cars overall and EVs in particular, has set targets to shift car sales away from gasoline-powered vehicles and has provided incentives to car companies and car buyers alike. Its initial target was for annual sales of new energy vehicles (NEVs) to reach 2 million by 2020. By 2025, it wants 7 million cars sold in China every year, or about 20 percent of the total, to be plug-in hybrids or battery powered, and it projects that a complete ban on sales of internal-combustion engines could occur before 2040.

Given that China is the world's largest car market, it's not surprising that immediately after China announced its mandate for NEVs, both General Motors and Ford released plans for major EV initiatives in coming years. Other car companies and governments around the world have followed suit. Just 2 to 3 billion EVs would mean that the world would need roughly five times the copper it consumes today. Current global reserve estimates for copper come nowhere close to this amount.

EVs aren't the only segment of the renewable-energy-related area that is copper intensive. So is solar and wind energy relative to fossil fuel energies.

Success in developing renewable energy has been impressive. Many analysts such as those with BP, the International Energy Agency, and others think that over the next 20 years or so, solar and wind could double their share of energy supplied to the world and might even account for virtually all the growth in power capacity in that time frame. This would mean that by 2040, renewables would account for nearly 50 percent of electrical generation and roughly 15 percent of total energy usage.

Great news. But there's at least one catch. Renewable energies require considerably more copper than fossil fuels do. It takes six tons of copper to create a megawatt of power from renewables compared to one ton for fossil fuels. Meanwhile, other uses for copper also would burgeon as urbanization in developing nations leads to more construction and more transmission of electricity.

I've done some rough but I think pretty accurate back-of-the-envelope calculations of what all this might imply through 2040. My calculations assume that the rate of copper growth for applications such as buildings, structures, and all others not directly related to energy will continue to grow in line with GDP growth. My estimate: adding it all up, worldwide demand for copper could grow two-and-a-half-fold to about 50 to 55 million metric tons a year. This equates to global copper consumption of roughly 1 billion metric tons over the next 20 years.

This exceeds the level of current copper reserves, which as of 2018 the United States Geological Survey pegs at 830 million metric tons. It's true that higher copper prices are likely to lead to higher reserve figures by spurring development of resources that currently aren't economical to develop. But here, too, there's a catch, one I referred to earlier: declining grades.

Declining Grades

In projecting copper's availability, you can't consider just the amount of copper ore being mined. You also have to take into account its grade—its relative richness—and how that affects costs in terms of both money and energy inputs. As grades decline, mining costs rise because it takes more energy to obtain a comparable amount of ore. And copper grades, indeed, have been in decline.

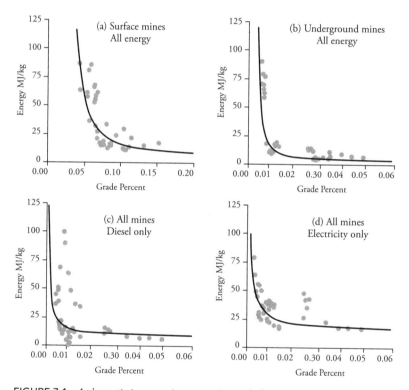

FIGURE 7.1 A dramatic increase in energy is needed as copper grades decline.

Source: From R. H. E. M. Koppelaar and H. Koppelaar, "The ore grade and depth influence on copper energy inputs." *Biophysical Economics and Resource Quantity* 2016; 1(2):1–16. Used with permission.

Worldwide copper grades, which used to average 5 to 10 percent per U.S. ton, have declined to 0.75 percent per ton. And this is just the average. In some cases, copper ore containing less than 0.5 percent per ton is being mined. This is copper's *inflection point*. Below 0.5 percent per ton, the amount of energy needed for mining jumps considerably. It continues to climb at an accelerating rate as the grade declines further. The fact that lower grades are now being mined is a major reason that real copper prices have risen sharply this century.

As more copper is needed for EVs and renewable-energy sources, it's a nearly sure bet that most newly developed copper mines will contain low grades. Extracting copper from such low-grade ore will be increasingly energy intensive and therefore costly. One implication is that as mining costs rise, copper prices will have to rise even more dramatically to make it feasible to add to reserves from existing resources. Price projections for copper going out five or more years will be far higher than almost anyone now expects.

I've spent some time talking about copper as a kind of case study illuminating the many intertwined factors that will affect the availability of commodities in coming years. But another commodity is even more central to the commodity story, and that's oil.

It's fair to say that a lot hinges on the outlook for oil. If oil supplies can rise to the occasion and match demand, commodity scarcities will be far less of a threat. But if oil scarcities emerge, as I expect they will, we're facing another kind of future entirely.

8
Oil, the Commodity King

Let me tell you something that we Israelis have against Moses.
He took us 40 years through the desert in order to bring us
to the one spot in the Middle East that has no oil!
—GOLDA MEIR

I MUST CONFESS that this quote isn't directly relevant to anything I'm about to discuss. But it's a great quote, and it does suggest the special role that oil plays in the world. After all, Meir wasn't bemoaning that Moses had brought the Israelis to a spot that lacked peanut butter.

In the pantheon of interrelated commodities that shape our world, oil occupies a special place. It's the commodity whose relative plenitude or scarcity will most determine whether overall commodity scarcities emerge and how quickly. This is because oil is still the most important energy source, and obtaining all commodities, including oil itself, requires a lot of energy.

If oil remains plentiful, then no worries. But if oil scarcities lie ahead, you should definitely be worrying—and starting to buy gold. And if on a worst-case basis we approach that dire game-over endpoint where to get oil requires using more oil than we obtain, you should be buying more gold.

Oil—often called *black gold*—is truly a critical commodity. It's an existential question whether we will run out of obtainable oil before achieving a full-scale transition from fossil fuels to renewable energy.

Note that I said *obtainable* oil. The world won't literally run out of oil. In a certain sense, oil is limitless, existing in places that we haven't begun to attempt to explore, much less tap, in the farthest reaches of the planet and perhaps beyond. Some of those areas may be feasible to explore and drill. But many more almost certainly won't be. And accessing the ones that can be tapped will require rising inputs not just of money but of oil itself.

Imagine all the ways oil gets pulled into the act if you hope to obtain oil from the remotest parts of Alaska. Oil is used in making the drilling equipment, in transporting and operating it, in transporting workers and building housing for them, in flying in food and other supplies, and in shipping the oil to refineries. Moreover, the more remote the area, the greater are the risks and costs of something going wrong, an accident in which huge amounts of the expensively obtained oil could be squandered within days.

Increasingly, the amount of oil you'd have to put into the effort would approach the amount you'd get out of it. At some point, it would surpass it.

In other words, for all practical purposes, oil is finite. This makes it urgent to act, before it's too late, to scale up the renewable energies such as wind and solar power, which are truly limitless. The urgency comes from the fact that transitioning to renewable—which involves such undertakings as building massive grids that transmit energy from disparate sources across big areas—will take a lot of energy. Will enough oil be there for us to succeed? Will we be smart enough to make effective use of the oil that remains available to us before it's too late?

Peak Oil and Energy Return on Investment

Perhaps you're familiar with the phrase *peak oil*, a phrase and notion that have been floating around for decades. Like many people, though, you may be under the impression that adherents to the theory of peak oil have been proven resoundingly wrong as oil has continued to flow, including via the putative success of hydraulic fracturing, better known as *fracking*.

Not so fast. In my opinion, peak oil is one of the most damaging phrases ever coined. Not because I believe that the notion is wrong—I don't. Rather, because of how it has been misinterpreted, which has made it unfortunately easy to discredit the notion of scarcities and therefore avoid doing something about them.

The concept of peak oil originated with Shell Oil researcher M. King Hubbert. As he defined it in the 1950s, it meant that once 50 percent of the original oil endowment of any area—whether an oil field, a region, a country, or the world—was extracted, oil production in that area would begin an irreversible decline. But that was never meant to suggest, as is often wrongly assumed, that production would then promptly start to go down or do so in a straight line.

Rather, the message is that once peak oil is reached, it starts to get more expensive both in money and in energy inputs either to maintain production at the same level or to raise it. To put it another way, the marginal costs of obtaining oil start to rise.

The anti–peak oil crowd, however, seems to believe that peak oil affirmers have claimed that oil production actually will level off or decline. They then have used that straw-man definition as evidence that peak oil is a delusion and that we needn't worry about scarcities. More recently, the abundant oil production from U.S. fracking is taken as proof that peak oil was nothing more than the ranting of dyspeptic geologists out to scare people with their unwarranted pessimistic vision.

But the complacency fostered by the seeming success of U.S. shale is dangerous. It overlooks that shale oil is more costly and more energy intensive than conventional oil and that the costs of extracting oil from shale will inevitably rise, to a point where no amount of money will suffice to obtain any meaningful amount of oil at all.

In retrospect, it would have been far better if instead of peak oil, Hubbert had talked about rising marginal costs. This gets at the heart of the issue. If we, meaning the United States, can focus on that issue, it would save us a lot of grief. So far there's no sign we're doing so.

In particular, it would be a huge step in the right direction if policymakers understood and took to heart a second concept: EROI, which stands for "energy return on investment" (or, alternatively, EROEI, for "energy return on energy invested"). This is a ratio that attempts to quantify the indisputable fact that it takes energy to get energy.

Charles A. S. Hall, an ecology systems scientist, came up with the term EROI in the 1970s and has written many books on the subject. In calculating how much oil gets used up in the extraction process, Hall included the kinds of factors I mentioned earlier plus additional considerations such as the oil that goes into the asphalt that makes the roads necessary to transport equipment, supplies, and workers.

EROI is the ratio of the number of barrels obtained to the number of barrels needed to obtain them once you take all such factors into account. The higher the ratio, the better. An EROI of 10 means that it takes 1 barrel of oil to get 10 barrels. This is obviously a lot better than using up 5 barrels of oil to get 10, an EROI of 2. A low EROI means both that oil is more expensive and that less net energy is left over to take care of all the things for which an economy needs oil. The lower the EROI, the harder it is to generate growth.

As EROI drops, at a certain point you're just spinning your wheels. When you get to a ratio of 1:1—when it takes a barrel of oil to get a barrel of oil—it's game over.

Hall concluded that it takes an EROI of at least 10 to meet the minimum requirements of society. To be a little more generous and supply a modern civilization with the cornucopia of goods and services it takes for granted, he estimated that an EROI of around 15 is needed.

The EROI ratio for fossil fuels has been in a gradual decline almost since the world first began using fossil fuels as an energy source. For a long time, though, this was essentially irrelevant because it was still so easy to get fossil fuels out of the ground. Lately, however, the decline in EROI has accelerated, making it a much more serious concern that can't be swatted away.

Today, the best estimate is that for the world at large, EROI is about 10. This means that around 10 percent of all energy being produced is consumed by the energy industry itself in order to obtain energy. But this is the average. It includes the huge amounts of oil from the Middle East, where oil flows relatively freely and EROI is far greater than 10.

Dragging the average down is oil being produced in areas such as the shale deposits in the United States, where frackers have been plying their trade. Shale oil is far more energy intensive to produce, with an EROI well below 10 and continuing to decline. If current trends continue, overall EROI will continue to drop. This tells you that there's good reason to worry about oil's availability as the century marches on.

Peak Demand?

Lately, there has been talk of *peak demand*, that is, that demand for oil will be leveling off. This is another reassuring-on-the-surface thought that you should quickly dismiss. It ignores oil's omnipresent role in the production of the gamut of commodities, demand for which will rise as the developing world pushes for growth.

A recent study published in the journal *Philosophical Transactions of the Royal Society* tackled the question of how much energy goes into producing other commodities. It came up with an estimate of about 8 percent.

Then pair this estimate with the projection from the International Energy Agency (IEA) that demand for commodities will double over the next 20 years. Looked at together, these two estimates portend a sharp increase in the demand for energy simply to produce commodities, never mind all the other things oil is needed for.

Keep in mind, too, that as discussed in Chapter 7, the grades of ore for many commodities are declining. As they continue to drop, the amount of oil needed to produce many commodities will increase. A 20 percent decline in the concentration of copper in a vein doubles the amount of energy needed to obtain the same amount of copper from a richer vein.

An argument frequently advanced to support the notion of peak demand is that oil demand will drop as EVs displace gasoline-powered cars. As I noted in Chapter 7, however, EVs require a lot more copper than gasoline-powered cars. The extra oil needed to obtain all that additional copper—especially as grades decline—will lessen net oil savings. Also, even as EVs grow in popularity, large numbers of gasoline-powered cars will remain on the road for many years.

Still, at some point, demand for gasoline will recede, possibly sharply, as we depend less directly on the fuel for our transportation needs. On a global basis, though, gasoline isn't the biggest source of oil demand. While in the United States gasoline accounts for 50 percent of oil usage, worldwide the figure is below 30 percent. Meanwhile, all the other ways oil is used will be burgeoning.

In particular, the fastest-growing uses of oil will be in petrochemicals, used in such diverse areas as agriculture, medicine, asphalt, construction, and more. By some estimates, high-income countries today on a per-capita basis use as much as 10 times more petrochemicals than lower-income countries do. This leaves a lot of room for petrochemical expansion as emerging economies build infrastructure and raise living standards.

And in yet another example of the complicated dynamics characterizing oil and energy, a major source of demand for petrochemicals, according to the IEA, will be the renewable-energy sector—for use in solar panels, wind turbines, batteries, and EVs.

Plastics, despite environmental concerns, have grown faster than any other bulk material, including cement, aluminum, and steel, according to the IEA. These other bulk materials also come with environmental issues. Steel and aluminum both require tremendous amounts of energy, and cement is water intensive. When it comes to commodities, there's no place to hide, no free lunch. They all are interdependent, and oil sits at the center of this nexus.

In all, I expect that over the next two decades, growth in petrochemical usage will average around 7 percent a year. Today, petrochemicals account for only around 11 percent of total oil demand. A generation from now I expect that they will account for well over 35 percent, one of many factors explaining why peak oil demand is a fantasy.

So Why Did the Oil Price Drop?

Okay, you may be thinking. Interesting discussion, interesting arguments, ingenious-sounding ratio, EROI. But still . . . if all this is true, if oil is growing scarcer and EROI is declining, then why did oil prices crash and burn—dropping nearly 80 percent—between mid-2014 and early 2016 despite worldwide growth? How could such a massive fall occur if the conditions for oil scarcities were unfolding?

The answer is that that period was anomalous. During that time, the oil market was flooded with extra supply. In the preceding years, fracking in the United States had taken off. Between 2011 and mid-2015, fracking added 4 million barrels a day to U.S. production. The Saudis weren't happy about all this extra oil coming online. Their solution was to have OPEC pump all out in an effort to deliberately push oil prices way down. The idea was that this would force many frackers, whose costs were high, out of business, putting control over the oil markets back in the hands of the Saudis.

Between March 2014 and the end of 2016, OPEC production rose by about 11 percent, or around 3 million additional barrels a day. The frackers were still continuing to produce as well, adding 4 million barrels a day. All this extra oil spilling into the market created a significant surplus of supply over demand, causing prices to swoon.

Two points are important here. One is that the surplus in oil at that time was misleading. It depended on the oil contributed by the frackers, and that oil was uneconomical to produce, with a relatively low EROI.

Moreover, the surge in supply came as the rate of growth in demand for oil had been slowing as the developing and developed worlds traded places. The Organisation for Economic Co-operation and Development (OECD) is a group of 34 democracies with free-market economies. It's a good stand-in for the high-income part of the world. In 2005, demand for oil by OECD countries started to decline. This is not surprising because developed economies, with larger service sectors, typically start to need less oil. Meanwhile, even though the developing world surpassed the developed world in 2011 in terms of overall economic size, it wasn't until 2013 that it surpassed it in demand for oil.

My aim in this chapter was to show that the world is facing oil scarcities, which will contribute to overall commodity scarcities and therefore to rising gold prices. But I need to nail down one more piece. I'm sure that you've noticed a hefty note of skepticism every time I mention fracking. If you've bought into the claim that fracking can keep us well supplied with oil for a long time to come, I hope that Chapter 9 will cause you to reconsider that rosy but faulty assumption.

9
Fracking Insanity

ITS BOOSTERS CELEBRATE fracking as the ticket to American energy independence and the savior of the U.S. economy. Its detractors excoriate it as a present and looming environmental catastrophe that is contaminating water supplies, spawning earthquakes, and releasing huge amounts of methane into the atmosphere, exacerbating global warming.

I call it a perfect example of short-term thinking, of America's disheartening penchant in the past half century to seize on short-term fixes rather than invest in longer-term goals. I'd also call it an example of why we're falling behind China when it comes to preparing for the future. And lastly, I'd call it another reason gold prices will rise.

Fracking, or hydraulic fracturing, is the technique of drilling horizontally through carbon-bearing rock. Fracking has made it possible to access gas and oil previously trapped in huge shale formations in Texas, Oklahoma, Pennsylvania, and some other parts of the country. Fracked oil, along with oil obtained from tar sands, is known as *unconventional* oil to distinguish it from the conventional oil produced by drilling holes in the ground.

Fracking began to really take off in the early part of the 2010s. It had long been known that areas of the United States, particularly the Southwest but also Pennsylvania, upstate New York, and elsewhere, sit atop deep layers of underground shale that is like a very hard sponge containing oil and natural gas in its pores. The question was how to tear the sponge apart to let the oil escape and come to the surface.

Fracking provided the answer. It's a multistep process that includes drilling down vertically, sometimes as much as 10,000 feet; encasing the drilled hole with cement to avoid water contamination; drilling horizontally into the shale layer for as much as a mile; and blasting it with massive amounts of water, sand, and various chemicals to create and widen fissures so that the oil can be brought to the surface.

The most prolific producer is the Permian Basin, straddling West Texas and New Mexico. Its unique geology includes layers of shale upon shale, making it extraordinarily fertile. From little more than a rounding error at the beginning of the decade, Permian production today accounts for about 60 percent of shale production and has been rising at a rate of more than 1 million barrels a day per year.

It's not surprising that many people believe that fracking has been a tremendous success. Since 2011, fracking has produced enough oil to boost U.S. oil production by more than 7 million barrels a day. It has resulted in a resurgence of U.S. oil production to the point where the United States has surpassed its oil production records of the 1970s. Amazingly, the United States has become the largest oil producer in the world, beating out Saudi Arabia and Russia.

Increases in natural gas production from shale, mostly from the Marcellus Shale formation, have been equally impressive. Indeed, America produces all the natural gas it can use and then some, and we've become a natural gas exporter—something few people would have believed possible a few years back.

In all, the seeming glories of fracking have led many, both on Wall Street and in the political sphere, to proclaim a new age of energy independence for the United States. It also has served to diminish any sense of urgency here about developing renewable energy to prepare for the day when oil production of any kind hits limits, as it inevitably will.

The problem is that fracking is mostly a chimera.

Warning Signs

One revealing sign that fracking isn't all it's cracked up to be is that almost without exception, frackers haven't made money, even from the prolific Permian Basin. Although they are taking money in from selling the oil they produce, they constantly need to borrow more just to keep the party going. Or, as economists would say, they are free-cash-flow negative. Several frackers have declared bankruptcy.

A particularly startling statistic is that according to the advisory firm Evercore ISI, as cited in a December 2017 article in the *Wall Street Journal*, over the preceding decade, energy companies spent $280 billion more on fracking than they made from it. Since 2011–2012, when fracking started in earnest, the frackers are more than a quarter of a trillion dollars in the hole.

Not surprisingly, shale has been a lousy bet for most investors. According to data provider FactSet, as the Standard and Poor's 500 Index (S&P 500) rose 80 percent, an index of U.S. producers fell 31 percent.

So how have the frackers kept going? By taking on debt. Banks have been happy to lay out money in the hope of a brighter future. They are betting on the Permian continuing to produce and to do so at an accelerating rate and cheaply enough that the frackers will eventually become dramatically free-cash-flow positive.

But prolific as the Permian is, from a financial standpoint, even this mammoth field is subject to the same considerations and restraints as less productive fields. The biggest players in the Permian may turn in positive free cash flows in 2018–2020, but no one expects that these cash flows will come anywhere close to making up for the billions and billions of dollars of investments that have gone into the Permian Basin.

It's not that the frackers are hapless incompetents. Their problems reflect the limits that are inherent in the nature of fracking. Fracked wells get depleted far more rapidly than conventional wells, with some experiencing 60 percent depletion within the first year of operation. Conventional wells and oil fields often can continue to produce for decades.

As a result, to keep production going, frackers must continually put money into developing new wells. This is why dedicated frackers like Chesapeake Energy (in gas) and Continental Resources (in oil) have seen capital expenditures rise considerably faster than fracking profits.

Energy Intensity

This isn't a problem just for the frackers themselves or for those who invest in them. It's a problem for all of us. The only truly meaningful question to ask about fracking is whether it can avert oil scarcities and, if so, for how long. Is it some magical, just-in-time gift that will keep on giving, keeping us awash in oil for a long time to come? The fact that frackers have had to continually invest more and more money just to keep production going is a strong indication that the answer is no.

Rapid well depletion is just one reason fracking is costly. Equally if not more important is that fracking is highly resource intensive. Massive quantities of liquids and sand and chemicals must be transported to fracking sites, wells must be cemented, waste disposed of, and huge amounts of diesel fuel brought in to run the heavy equipment. Once oil is produced, it must be transported to refineries, whether via pipelines or by trucks.

Oil is critical to all these processes. And that circles back to the concept of EROI, energy return on investment. To evaluate the contribution made by fracking—to determine how much extra oil it is contributing to the economy—you can't look just at one-half of the equation, the oil released from shale. You also have to take into account how much oil gets used up in the process. When you do so, the net energy gained from fracking looks increasingly underwhelming.

There are a lot of pertinent statistics that point to fracking being to some extent a sleight of hand, a matter of robbing Peter to pay Paul. Some of the data has to do with something called energy intensity.

Energy intensity measures how much energy an economy uses per unit of gross domestic product (GDP). An economy with high energy intensity expends a lot of energy in order to generate growth. An economy with low energy intensity gets by with less energy per unit of growth, a more desirable scenario.

Energy intensity in the United States has been rising sharply since the early part of this decade. This is worrisome, and it shouldn't be happening. Like all highly developed economies, the United States generates most of its GDP—around 80 percent—from its service sector. This should mean a decline in energy intensity because the service sector is far less energy intensive than the manufacturing and resource extraction sectors that dominate in less developed economies. And indeed, earlier this century, energy intensity in the United States was in a consistent downtrend.

Starting around 2012, however, this changed. For the five years ending in 2017, U.S. GDP grew at an average annualized rate of 2.17 percent, while oil consumption rose by about 1.7 percent a year. In other words, during this five-year period, it took 78 percent of a barrel of oil to generate about 1 percent of GDP growth (1.7/2.17). This was roughly on a par with the developing world, including China and India. Meanwhile, during that same period, many European countries, admittedly with somewhat less growth than the United States, saw oil consumption decline.

No matter how you adjust for growth, the rise in U.S. oil consumption relative to GDP over the past five years is a striking outlier. After starting the decade with oil consumption declining while GDP was growing, suddenly this most developed country is using nearly as much oil relative to GDP as in the very early 1970s. This is remarkable when you think how in that era oil was plentiful and cheap, meaning that there was little monetary incentive to use it efficiently.

The usual suspects don't explain it. For example, Americans have been driving a bit more this decade, but more fuel-efficient cars compensate for the additional miles.

What changed? The most notable change is that fracking began to surge. And with consumer usage of gasoline and other oil products relatively flat, by far the most plausible explanation for rising energy intensity here is that more and more oil is being diverted to fracking.

Out of Whack

Let's look at this from a slightly different angle with an additional set of statistics. In roughly the first decade and a half of this century (through 2015), oil production in the United States climbed by a bit less than 50 percent, to 8.4 million barrels a day. Natural gas production increased by a similar percentage, whereas coal production declined by about 15 percent. Overall energy production in America rose by about 45 percent.

During the same period, the value the energy sector added directly to GDP climbed more than fourfold. In other words, the energy sector ballooned. It constituted an increasingly large part of the overall economy—but it didn't produce an amount of extra energy commensurate with that gain in size. The energy sector grew fourfold but produced only 50 percent more energy.

Energy is most effective in boosting GDP when the bulk of its contribution is indirect, that is, as a power source for virtually every aspect of the economy—from cars, trucks, and home appliances to even smartphones.

The more energy's relationship to GDP is direct—meaning the energy sector and energy production as a proportion of GDP—rather than indirect, the less positive it is for the economy and for GDP growth. Imagine if energy production accounted for nearly 100 percent of our economic output. This would mean that the economy would effectively shut down because the greater the portion of the economy dedicated to energy production, the less is available for using energy for other sources. Another way of putting this is that the more energy we need to create energy, the worse off we are.

This helps explain something many people found puzzling. In 2014–2016, when oil prices fell, it didn't juice up the economy, as happened in past periods of falling oil prices. It's a truism that higher oil prices function as a kind of a tax, cutting into disposable income and making consumers more hesitant to spend. Thus, when starting in 2014 oil prices dropped by 70 percent, it should have been a tremendous boon to the economy. But it wasn't. Instead, we had trouble avoiding recession.

The explanation is that lower oil prices hurt the energy industry itself. Some frackers shut down altogether, with ripple effects on suppliers and all their employees. It was a clear illustration of just how big a part of the overall economy the energy sector has become. This helps explain why it has been responsible for diverting so much energy to its own operations and why the United States, in contrast to other developed economies, has not experienced a decline in energy intensity.

Short-Changing Renewables

Fracking is a road to nowhere. It produces less net oil than is generally realized and will be producing even less as time goes on. Lately, producers have been opening new wells known as *baby* wells that are located near existing wells. These baby wells essentially cannibalize some of the production from the parent well rather than tapping into previously untapped pools of oil.

But there's another serious knock against fracking. It has let us take our eyes off what we should be pursuing with fanatic purpose—the scaling up of wind and solar and other renewable-energy sources.

Mostly when you hear how urgent it is to focus on renewables, the focus is on the dangers of climate change and global warming. The need to confront climate change is urgent—and, by the way, its effects, from relocating millions of displaced people to rebuilding ravaged cities, will further add to the demand for energy. But you could even think that climate change is a hoax and still believe in the urgency of scaling up renewables based on the prospects for oil scarcities alone. If we wait until those scarcities are upon us, we will have missed the boat.

Thinking that fracking lets us off the hook is a grievous mistake. Oil will remain the world's major energy source for a while, but scarcities will emerge, and fracking won't ward them off. We should view whatever extra oil we can produce now as a welcome gift that lets us concentrate on the alternative energy sources that increasingly will be essential in replacing oil when our window of opportunity closes. Unfortunately, the United States isn't dedicating itself to that effort with nearly enough sense of urgency.

In the United States, many of the initiatives to develop renewable energy have come from state regulations aimed at cutting carbon emissions. Their goal has been clean energy, not tackling energy scarcity, but whatever the purpose, the initiatives are welcome. But such an effort doesn't do away with the need for a nationwide all-out push to develop renewable-energy infrastructure on a larger scale.

While the United States lacks a coherent renewable-energy policy, China and the E.U. countries have been moving ahead. China dominates renewable energy, including storage solutions such as batteries, solar modules, nuclear technologies, and perhaps most important, grid technologies. In 2017, China spent around 2.5 times what the United States did on renewables. It spent more than three times as much as the United States on the most important renewable, solar energy. China accounted for 40 percent of global spending on renewables.

The big challenge with wind and solar energy has always been storage. It's estimated that in one hour, enough sun hits the Earth to meet the world's energy needs for a year. But it's not available everywhere at all times. Similarly, wind has enormous potential: turbines on a relatively small portion of the Earth's land plus offshore turbines could meet all the planet's energy needs. But you can't count on the wind to blow. Storage solutions such as batteries don't make enough of a dent to solve the problem.

A more promising approach, one that could mostly circumvent the storage problem, would be a massive electric grid able to transmit energy almost instantaneously from a locale where the sun is shining or the wind is blowing to far-off regions connected to the grid. In conjunction with metering, specialized circuit breakers, and logistic algorithms, this is the essence of a *smart grid*. The more time zones such a grid could traverse, the better—potentially encircling the world.

Such a grid requires ultra-high-voltage direct-current (UHVDC) cables. As we discussed previously, China's grid today consists of about 15,000 miles of UHVDC cable. How many miles does the United States have? As of now, zero!

When China completes its grid, which will be the backbone for all its electrical needs including EVs and smart highways, it will have spent more than $1 trillion on it. This is more than twice what the United States spent to create our interstate highway system in today's dollars. Spending that can take full advantage of the grid will be measured in the trillions of dollars.

If all it took were money, we still might be able to catch up, assuming that we had the will and determination to do so. China, though, has an additional edge over us beyond its big head start: its government can mandate that the grid span the entire country. It's more complicated in the United States, where every state has its own zoning regulations. Under the rosiest assumptions, it would take at least a decade for the United States to get to where China is today, by which time China will have moved even further along.

Where does this leave the United States? One possibility would be to work with China. It wants to share the wealth—for a price. The country has begun to export its grid technology as well as its solar and wind technologies to others, especially in the East. Its stated long-term goal is a $50 trillion worldwide grid it hopes to complete, with the help of other countries, by midcentury.

Whether we choose to use China's technology or develop our own, one certainty is that fracking isn't the answer. A second certainty is that if we don't find a better answer soon, we'll be ruing our complacency for a long time to come.

10

Why China Wants to Dethrone the Dollar

CENTURIES AGO, JOHANN Wolfgang Von Goethe noted, "It's in the anomalies that nature reveals its secrets." I'm a big believer in the illuminating power of anomalies. If something stands out as odd, it's a strong clue that below the surface things are happening that cry out for investigation, whether in science, the investment arena, or anywhere else.

A while back, an anomaly began to nag at me: China's all-out efforts to mine its own gold. For more than a decade, China has been by far the world's biggest gold miner, producing about 400 tons a year on average. Its output in 2018, according to the United States Geological Survey, was 400 tons. This easily outstripped the next biggest producer, Australia, which mined 310 tons.

What makes this odd, or anomalous, is that China mines more than 13 percent of the world's gold despite having less than 4 percent of global reserves. For any commodity, while reserves overall can be mined economically, mining costs increase as reserves get extracted. So typically, based on economic calculations, you'd rein in your mining activities at a certain point. But China hasn't done so.

In 2018, China mined 20 percent of its reserves. This not only was the highest percentage for any gold miner, but it was also roughly equal to the highest percentage of reserves mined for any commodity in any year other than for China's own gold mining in the recent past. For comparison, whereas Russia also has been frantically adding to its gold holdings, it has been mining only about 5 percent of its reserves.

In other words, 20 percent is an extreme outlier. It suggests both that mining costs are high and that China nonetheless is mining an amount of gold that is historically large when viewed against mining history across all commodities. It is equivalent to a baseball player hitting more than 100 home runs in a season or batting close to .500.

I was at a loss to explain what was going on until several years ago, serendipitously, I was pointed to the answer. I was having lunch with a well-placed Harvard-educated Chinese asset manager. She had heard me speak at an investment conference in New York and had contacted me to discuss some investment possibilities she had in mind.

Somewhat idly, I asked her why China was mining so much gold. Her off-the-cuff response was that China needed lots of gold so as to back its currency, the yuan.

I found that startling. Back then, I hadn't yet considered such a possibility. I pressed her for further details.

She backtracked, as if realizing she had been indiscreet. No, no, she said, she had misspoken. What she had meant to say was that China was mining so much gold because the Chinese are so fond of gold jewelry. While it's certainly true that the Chinese prize gold jewelry, it seemed clear that her initial response had been more honest.

That eye-opening conversation, a casual throwaway, retracted remark, on its own wouldn't have been enough to convince me that China had plans to back or otherwise link its currency with gold or in some manner use gold to dethrone the dollar as the world's primary reserve currency. But the conversation was a spark, a starting point. It helped put subsequent moves by China in context and clarify where they pointed.

China's steady accumulation of gold has not slowed. Today, even as it keeps importing massive amounts of gold, China continues to be the world's largest gold miner, unearthing a larger percentage of its reserves than any country has ever mined of any commodity ever. Such activity bespeaks a country obsessed with the goal of acquiring every ounce of gold it possibly can. And it is not simply to satisfy its citizens' love of jewelry.

In earlier chapters I focused on forthcoming commodity scarcities as one pillar that will support gold's rise. But the second pillar—a new monetary system backed by gold—is even more central to understanding why gold will soar.

China has many reasons to want to create such a system and diminish the clout of the dollar. From China's perspective, the dollar's primacy is a holdover from a world that no longer exists. It allows the United States to continue to enjoy privileges that it no longer merits while ignoring China's rise and importance to the global economy. It also hands the United States the ability to bully other nations by imposing sanctions on them any time it chooses.

Beyond this, China sees the dollar's continued primacy as dangerous, unable to ensure a stable global system, something that the 2008 financial crisis revealed with devastating clarity.

But dethroning the dollar won't be easy. For a new system to succeed, the link to gold is essential. In accumulating gold, China is both signaling its intention to put such a new monetary system into place and laying the necessary foundation to do so.

Bretton Woods and After

Let's quickly review the history of the current monetary system, under which the U.S. dollar is the dominant currency throughout the world. Almost all international trade is conducted in dollars, and central banks throughout the world hold large quantities of dollars as foreign reserves.

The dollar's primacy was enshrined at the 1944 Bretton Woods Conference that established the postwar financial order. At the time, there was no question that if a single sovereign currency would be picked as the world's primary reserve currency, it would be the U.S. dollar. The United States had emerged from World War II with the world's largest military. Its economy was the world's biggest. It conducted more international trade than any other country. It checked all the relevant boxes, with no other country coming close.

This didn't mean that everyone thought basing the system on a single currency, even the U.S. dollar, was such a hot idea. One fierce opponent was British economist John Maynard Keynes. He argued that a unit based on a collection of commodities, which he dubbed the *bancor*, would be a better approach. But his side lost the argument.

When the new system was being thrashed out, the United States had another advantage along with the ones just mentioned. The new reserve currency would be backed by gold, and the United States possessed the most gold, an estimated 20,000 tons. This made it credible when the United States agreed to back the dollar with gold at the fixed price of $35 an ounce. Any country at any time could hand over dollars to the United States and receive gold in return.

This guarantee ended in 1971 when President Nixon delinked the dollar from gold. He really had no choice. To fund the Vietnam War and still maintain domestic spending, the United States was printing so many dollars that it didn't have the gold to back them up, not at $35 an ounce. But even after being delinked from gold, essentially unraveling one strand of Bretton Woods, the dollar held onto its role as the world's primary reserve currency.

This was partly because the United States still had the largest economy and most powerful military. But what really sealed the deal was the arrangement Nixon forged with the Saudis. They would price oil in dollars—hence the term *petrodollars*—in exchange for which the Saudis and the Saudi monarchy could count on the United States for military protection. From the 1970s on, through thick and thin, the dollar's unique connection to oil and, by extension, to all commodities ensured that the dollar would remain the world's primary currency.

With oil priced in dollars, every country needed dollars to purchase oil and other commodities, things no country could do without. This meant that demand for the dollar was guaranteed, and with the dollar therefore seen as completely safe, it meant that there would always be a market for U.S. debt. A further perk was that relative to inflation, we never had to pay excessive interest rates.

Even in the 1970s and early 1980s, when we had double-digit inflation, we had no trouble selling our debt. This dynamic has persisted to this day: in the wake of the 2008 financial crisis, U.S. dollars continued to be seen as a safe haven. Nor did we ever risk spiraling into the kind of hyperinflation that has ravaged other countries. This ability to attract lenders without having to worry about maintaining any sort of fiscal discipline was famously dubbed *exorbitant privilege* by French President Valery Giscard d'Estaing. It gave the United States flexibility that no other country had to issue debt with abandon, as indeed we did, without worrying about having to pay the piper.

China's Perspective

While the dollar has continued to hang onto its position as the primary global currency, today the rationale is less clear-cut. Those three boxes that the United States checked back in 1944 that made it the obvious choice to have the reserve currency—the biggest economy, the biggest trader, and the strongest military? Today, China can plausibly lay claim to all three.

■ **The economy.** In terms of purchasing power parity, China's economy exceeds ours. And you even could argue, as I do in Chapter 18, that because of the way the United States has consistently understated inflation, China's economy, even when measured in purely dollar terms, is closer in size to ours than is believed and will surpass ours in dollar size sooner than believed.

■ **Trade.** China is the world's biggest trader. In 2018, Chinese exports, at nearly $2.5 trillion, amounted to 13 percent of the world's total. Its imports, at $2.15 trillion, were 11 percent of the world's total.

■ **The military.** Yes, even when it comes to military might, where the United States is assumed to have an unassailable lead, major cracks have started to appear. The United States outspends China both in dollars and as a percentage of gross domestic product, but China's spending is more efficient (as is true of its infrastructure spending) and more focused on China's specific objectives.

The United States has the military firepower to win a world war, should such an awful conflict erupt. But China isn't trying to compete on that playing field. Its rapidly expanding military is geared first toward security of its own territory and second toward the security of Eastern countries, including those within the Belt and Road Initiative (BRI). Moreover, China has an edge because of its access to and control over rare earth minerals, which are critical to much of the most advanced military technology.

Don't get me wrong. The United States is still an immensely powerful country that holds numerous cards, one of which is the dollar's continued status as the world's primary reserve currency. Two basic measures of the dollar's dominance are the proportion of international trade conducted in dollars and the proportion of foreign reserves that central banks hold in dollars. As of 2018, according to the International Monetary Fund (IMF), the U.S. dollar makes up two-thirds of global reserve holdings and is used in about 60 percent of trade. Also bolstering the dollar's continued hold, oil and other essential commodities continue to be priced in dollars (something China also is working to challenge). Having been entrenched for so long, the dollar still has a lot going for it. It won't be dislodged overnight.

But to assume that the dollar will stay on top forever is to be blissfully complacent. You can view the world today as being in an evolving push-pull moment between past and present, West and East, twentieth century and twenty-first century. What's indisputable is that in this century, power and influence have been flowing east. China's enormous economy, its huge investments in infrastructure in the expanding BRI arena—encompassing more than half the world's population—and its rising share of international trade all are manifestations of this shift.

Thus it is easy to understand why China wants a role in the global monetary infrastructure commensurate with its rising economic profile. It's particularly understandable that China would chafe at the dollar remaining the currency used in China's own trade with BRI countries and other developing nations, countries that depend more on China than on the United States

The Triffin Dilemma

If China intends to dethrone the dollar, some immediate questions include the following: What does it want to put in the dollar's place? How likely is it to succeed? How fast could it happen? And how and why will gold be part of the process?

My quick-form answers: While internationalizing the yuan is an important initial step, China isn't looking to simply replace the dollar with the yuan. Rather, its ultimate vision is of a basket of currencies that includes the yuan in a prominent role alongside the dollar and selected other currencies and, crucially, that is linked with gold.

I'd rate the chance of China succeeding as, oh, I don't know, 100 percent. And I think that the shift could happen sooner than is expected even by those who concede that at some point the dollar inevitably will yield its current role.

It's important to understand that China doesn't simply want to replace the dollar with the yuan as the world's primary reserve currency. Why doesn't it? Because in the eyes of China's leaders, a monetary reserve system based on *any* single sovereign currency is inherently flawed. A basket of currencies, backed by gold, would address those flaws, in China's eyes better serving not just China's interests but the world's.

I noted earlier that at Bretton Woods not everyone thought it wise to have a single sovereign currency serve as a reserve currency. The issue was vigorously debated, with Keynes a leading opponent. But the position of the United States in favor of the dollar held sway. And, for a while, the system worked as it was supposed to, providing plenty of liquidity for international trade without leading to distortions in the form of an overvalued dollar.

By the late 1960s, however, an underlying problem with the existing system was becoming more evident. It is known as *Triffin's dilemma*, after Belgian-American economist Robert Triffin. Triffin, as far back as 1959, testifying before the U.S. Congress, had identified an inherent conflict when a sovereign currency such as the dollar must simultaneously do two different things: meet domestic monetary goals while, at the same time, supplying enough liquidity to grease the wheels of international trade.

If the U.S. central bank, the Federal Reserve, wants to fight inflation through tighter monetary policy, it risks supplying too few dollars to the world to support global growth. By contrast, if it provides too much stimulus at home, it would likely raise U.S. long-term interest rates, causing the dollar to become increasingly overvalued as more foreign money pours into higher-yielding U.S. bonds.

This risks setting off a vicious circle in which domestic inflation feeds on itself. Greater domestic spending leads to rising imports and a higher trade deficit. The trade deficit, in turn, must be financed with increased borrowing. The result is still higher long-term interest rates, more spending, more borrowing, and so on.

The dollar's overvaluation reflects the reality that other countries need dollars to conduct trade, including buying essentials such as oil. This allows dollar bonds to offer somewhat lower rates than bonds of other countries.

Moreover, the United States doesn't get punished for the high inflation that might ensue if it overstimulates its economy. Long-term rates will rise, but if anything, the higher yields may enhance the dollar's appeal. In the late 1970s and early 1980s, when U.S. inflation rose to double digits, the dollar dipped but by far less than had it not been the world's reserve currency. In other words, it remained overvalued.

In other countries, high inflation usually deals a killer blow to the currency, likely leading to highly restrictive monetary policy, a recession, and an IMF bailout. As most economists acknowledge, the dollar's chronic overvaluation stemming from its reserve currency role is the chief reason for the trade deficits the United States has run with other countries.

The 2008 global economic crisis crystallized for China's leaders the problems with the existing monetary reserve system. The crisis arose from failings in the West that had nothing to do with China. Namely, it stemmed from the collapse of the U.S. housing market and the effect on U.S. financial institutions that had issued risky and complex financial instruments based on the airy assumption that housing prices could never fall.

At its height, the turmoil in U.S. financial markets was so great that AAA borrowers were on the verge of skipping payrolls for lack of short-term borrowing facilities. Given the importance of dollars in international transactions, it is not hard to imagine that the world's entire financial structure was on the verge of collapse. Dollars became extremely scarce.

As the repercussions swept through the world, dragging down global growth and pushing the United States into the worst recession since the Great Depression, China responded by spending massive amounts of money to keep its own economy growing. China's efforts helped prop up the rest of the world, preventing the economic debacle from being even worse than it was by creating Chinese demand for commodities and goods produced elsewhere. But China's actions also led to rising debt in China and contributed to corruption.

The experience reinforced the view of Chinese leaders that as long as the dollar was the backbone of international trade, China's economy, and the global economy at large, would remain at the mercy of the United States and the West and could be whipsawed at any time by poor decisions and profligacy half a world away. This went directly contrary to China's determination to control its own fate as it seeks to improve the welfare of Chinese citizens. China's economic growth, making it possible to lift some 800 million Chinese out of poverty in the past 30 years, is the underlying justification for the Communist's Party's tight control over society. Keeping growth going is part of the basic bargain the party has made with the Chinese people. The dollar's continuing hegemony risks undermining that bargain at any time.

Zhou's 2009 Essay

An essay written in March 2009 by Zhou Xiaochuan offers an illuminating window into China's thinking about a new reserve currency—and why it should be backed by gold. When he wrote it, Zhou was serving his second five-year term as head of China's central reserve bank, the People's Bank of China (PBOC). Fluent in English (he studied for two years at the University of California at Santa Cruz) and known for his friendships with Westerners, including former U.S. Treasury Secretary Henry Paulson, Zhou has been immensely consequential in China's emergence this century and in making its economy more market oriented. It was a testament to Zhou's abilities and political skills that although he had been widely expected to step down in 2012 when his term ended, President Xi appointed him to a third five-year term, making Zhou at the time the longest-serving head of any major central bank.

His 2009 essay, which cited the Triffin dilemma, was a concise analysis of the problems he saw with the existing monetary reserve system and pointed to the kind of system China would prefer in its place. It did not mention gold by name. But it hinted strongly, without too much reading between the lines, that a new system should be anchored to gold.

The 2008 financial crisis and its aftermath, Zhou wrote, confronted the world with a "long-existing but still unanswered question, i.e., what kind of international reserve currency do we need to secure global financial stability and facilitate world economic growth?"

He continued: "The crisis again calls for creative reform of the existing international monetary system towards an international reserve currency with a stable value, rule-based issuance and manageable supply, so as to achieve the objective of safeguarding global economic and financial stability."

Zhou homed in on a basket of reserve assets called *special drawing rights* (SDRs). The IMF had created SDRs in 1969 as a way to add liquidity to global trade. SDRs are not a currency per se. Rather, they represent a claim to currencies held by IMF member countries and constitute a supplementary form of foreign exchange reserve asset that central banks can hold. SDRs are administered by the IMF, and only governments, not private individuals or companies, can use them.

In the passage where he clearly was referring to gold, Zhou wrote: "The allocation of the SDR can be shifted . . . to a system backed by real assets . . . to further boost market confidence in its value." Focus on the words *backed by real assets*.

Why could this only mean gold? Because gold is the only real asset that would qualify. Remember, gold is unique among real assets in not being used up over time. Virtually every ounce of gold ever mined still exists on the planet. Any other asset would create insurmountable accounting problems as its supply shrank.

Zhou probably was careful not to mention gold explicitly because that would have drawn attention to China's sub rosa accumulation of the metal, which continued to accelerate sharply after 2009. China, with its long-game mentality, wanted to keep that under wraps for a while.

When Zhou wrote his essay in 2009, the SDR was comprised of just four currencies, all of which were part of the basket at its inception and that were weighted in the SDR units according to their importance in international trade. They were the U.S. dollar, the euro, the British pound sterling, and the Japanese yen.

In November 2015, China scored a major triumph, one that Zhou had sought for years. At its regular five-year review of the composition of the SDR, the IMF announced that it would add China's yuan as a fifth currency. The yuan actually was awarded a higher weighting, at 10.92 percent, than both the yen (8.33 percent) and the pound sterling (6.09 percent). The dollar led at 41.73 percent, followed by the euro at 30.93 percent. The yuan officially joined the SDR in October 2016.

The consensus among Western analysts was that the IMF's decision was a symbolic win for China that acknowledged the country's economic importance but that it meant little in practical terms. One reason was that while the SDR had been around for a while, its role as a reserve currency was only an auxiliary one. And while the Chinese yuan, once it was included in the SDR, gained some traction as a global reserve currency, its portion was very small—just 1.1 percent of global reserve currency holdings by the third quarter of 2017. Once again, however, you need to remember that China plays the long game. Getting its foot, that is, the yuan, in the door of the SDR currency was never meant to be more than an early step, a building block, toward something more.

Returning to Zhou's essay, written years before the yuan joined the SDR, one of Zhou's recommendations was that the SDR be expanded and given a much larger, more central role in global trade. An SDR that included many more currencies as well as gold backing would be a natural unit to supplant the dollar.

The Power to Sanction

There is another big reason that China—and other countries, too—would happily dethrone the dollar. The dollar's role as the global reserve currency, the currency all other countries need to conduct international trade and, in particular, to purchase oil, is what lets the United States impose and enforce sanctions on other countries and individuals. The United States has wielded this power with a free hand to punish financial crimes and in pursuit of geopolitical goals, and of late, it has been doing so with even more abandon, including targeting Chinese companies and individuals.

The payment system governing transactions between different governments and companies domiciled in different countries is complex. Every country has its own protocols for transferring monies within the banks of that country. What allows those intracountry protocols to mesh with one another is the Society for Worldwide Interbank

Financial Telecommunications (SWIFT), access to which is needed to conduct most foreign trading. SWIFT enables the United States to keep track of the flow of dollars, revealing any violations of sanctions. This makes it essentially impossible for a country, company, or individual to defy sanctions without being detected and risk having its own dollar assets in U.S. banks frozen.

An office within the U.S. Treasury Department, the Office of Foreign Assets Control (OFAC), is responsible for issuing and monitoring sanctions. The office was created in 1950 as a successor to an agency that had imposed sanctions on Germans before and doing World War II. An interesting historical footnote is that the first country to be the target of sanctions by OFAC was China, along with North Korea, in 1950 when China entered the Korean War on the side of North Korea.

In the age of Trump, even America's allies have gotten fed up with some of the ways the United States has used the dollar's privileged status to push U.S. policies. In particular, after the United States withdrew from the Iran nuclear deal and reimposed sanctions on Iran, European countries remaining in the deal have sought workarounds that would let them continue to trade with Iran in defiance of the sanctions. But it has been tough to find workable solutions.

"Chinese Dream"

Bringing in gold is an inextricable part of China's plans to remake the monetary system. China's continued frenetic mining and overall accumulation of gold point to this and is crucial in aiding China to shape a new monetary system and be its major beneficiary.

The significance of China's gold holdings is what's missing from the analysis of Western commentators who recognize China's desire to dethrone the dollar but argue that it won't happen anytime soon. They point to the dollar still being the overwhelmingly predominant currency whether you're looking at reserves, international trade, or international debt. In addition, they point to China's still relatively unliberalized economy—a valid point, but something China knows it has to address. The yuan, they say, simply can't vie with the dollar's entrenched advantage. And they might have been right—if not for the gold factor.

Song Xin is China's "Mr. Gold." He's president of the China Gold Association, chairman of the Chinese International Resource Corporation, chairman of the state-owned China National Gold Corporation, and Party Secretary for gold. In other words, he's the most important liaison between the gold industry and the Chinese government.

In 2014, Song said:

> For China, gold's strategic mission is to support the internationalization of the renminbi and be a strong support for China's goals of becoming an economic power and realizing the "Chinese Dream."
>
> Gold is the only product that holds properties of a commodity and currency; it's the most trusty asset on which modern fiat currency can be based. From a historical perspective, gold has played an irreplaceable role in times of financial and geopolitical crises and in protecting a country's economic security. It is this unique nature and function of gold that give it a glorious and holy role to play during the revitalization of the greatness of the Chinese people and the realization of the "Chinese Dream."

China's accumulation of gold is one portent of the country's intention to push the dollar off its singular throne and midwife a new monetary system linked to gold. With its long-term perspective and ability to play possum for as long as it's useful, China isn't trumpeting its gold holdings or bringing them into play just yet. But inevitably it will.

11

The Eastern Oil Benchmark

WHEN LATER THIS century historians relate, as they will, how the dollar lost its role as the world's primary reserve currency, one date they are sure to note is March 26, 2018. This was the day China launched an Eastern oil benchmark denominated in yuan. A long-planned and often-delayed move, it wasn't intended to shrink the dollar's role or elevate the yuan or gold overnight, and it didn't. But it was a significant step forward toward those goals.

Remember, ever since Nixon, oil priced in dollars has been a linchpin of the dollar's continued reign as the world's chief reserve currency. Oil is the world's most traded commodity, essential to economies around the world. As long as countries need dollars to obtain oil, the dollar's reserve currency status is safe. But once oil, in meaningful amounts, is priced and traded in another currency, it opens the gates to a new era.

Chapter 10 discussed why China is eager to replace the dollar-based system with one based on a basket of currencies linked to gold. But China isn't prone to wishful thinking. It doesn't merely aspire to remake the monetary reserve system. It has a plan for how to get there and has already taken concrete steps to do so. China's burgeoning presence in oil markets is part of that effort.

Gold, it turns out, isn't the only thing China has been accumulating. It also has been frantically importing and stockpiling oil, part of its effort to set up the game board in ways that will let it dictate the rules of a new monetary order. Oil, which still is the world's most important commodity, is crucial to that effort. So are connections China is forging that link oil, gold, and the yuan with one another. Some of these links are somewhat opaque, making this an example of connecting several not-so-obvious dots.

Oil Stockpiling and More

In 2017, China became the world's biggest importer of oil, surpassing the United States But that's just one aspect of China's oil activities. It has been stockpiling massive amounts of oil, has rapidly built up the country's refining capabilities, and, as noted earlier, has launched an Eastern oil benchmark denominated in yuan.

China's stockpiling of oil into its strategic reserves has been relentless. According to the U.S. Energy Information Administration (EIA) and other sources, in 2014, China added around 20,000 barrels of oil a month to its reserves. The following year, the figure leapt to 289,000 barrels a month. In 2016, it rose further to 470,000 barrels a month. By then Chinese stockpiling was accounting for around 31 percent of global growth in oil demand.

Many analysts expected that 2016 would prove the apex and that growth in China's oil stockpiling would thereafter slump, leading to a global drop in oil demand. But neither of those things happened. In the first nine months of 2018, China added about 200 million barrels of crude. This must have surprised oil analysts: in early 2017, the IEA had projected that China was running out of storage space, with room for only an additional 150 million barrels. But China's stockpiling has continued.

What explains China's urgent push to accumulate ever more oil? One reason, I think, is that it reflects China's assessment of the supply/demand dynamics for the commodity. Unlike most analysts in the West, China foresees a gap opening up between oil demand and supply that will send prices soaring. It wants to make sure to have enough oil on hand to meet all its needs before that happens.

Most Western analysts expect oil demand to rise only modestly in the coming decade and beyond. The general assumption is that daily demand will rise on average by less than 1 million barrels a year through 2030. After that, some analysts think that demand will continue to grow through 2040 before plateauing and then starting to decline. Others expect that demand will plateau sooner, closer to 2030. Whatever the timeline, the thinking is that rising sales of electric vehicles (EVs), along with greater reliance on wind, solar, and other alternative energy sources, will rein in oil demand.

But this analysis is overly simplistic. Take EVs, for instance. As I discussed in Chapter 8 while EVs might seem like the answer to gas-guzzling vehicles, it will take a while before they have a real impact on gasoline demand. And even as transportation-related demand for oil slows, demand for oil for use in petrochemicals will be soaring. Oil is the feedstock for petrochemicals, which are processed into a huge array of products used in everyday life, including plastics, fertilizers, textiles, solvents, medicines, and more. Demand for all these items will be rising sharply in developing countries.

In fact, demand for oil for use in petrochemicals could easily raise overall demand for oil well above what is generally expected for at least another generation. Some analysts argue that we can find alternatives for most oil-based chemicals. But it's not that simple.

In an April 2019 article in Science magazine, Phil de Luna and coauthors looked at what it would take for electrosynthesis powered by renewable energy to replace petrochemical processes, one alternative that has been suggested. The authors concluded that the effort would require electrical-to-chemical conversion efficiencies of at least 60 percent—chemistry that is beyond today's capabilities. Moreover, obtaining the renewable energy to power the process would require new infrastructure that in itself would require a lot of oil.

China seems to understand that for the foreseeable future, growth in oil demand will likely continue at its current pace or even accelerate somewhat. Eventually, demand for oil will start to subside. But the time frame for that to happen likely will be longer than generally believed.

Besides stockpiling oil, China also has been dramatically boosting its capacity to refine crude oil into gasoline, diesel fuel, and petrochemicals. The United States is still the world's biggest refiner, with a capacity of around 18 million barrels a day. Over the past decade, though, production has stagnated at around that level. If China's refining capacity continues to grow as expected, China will catch up to the United States early this decade and by the middle of the decade will be far ahead.

This will position China to be the dominant supplier of refined oil to much of the East and the emerging world, oil that will be the feedstock for most organic chemicals. China already is the world's largest exporter of inorganic chemicals.

And then there's China's launch in March 2018 of an Eastern oil benchmark denominated in yuan. It is likely to prove to be a watershed event with ramifications that will extend well beyond oil.

Benchmarks Old and New

Oil prices, obviously, are enormously important to the global economy and to financial markets, and financial analysts follow them closely. When you hear that oil is at a certain price on any given day, the reference is to its price on one of two Western oil benchmarks: West Texas Intermediate (WTI) in the United States and Brent in Europe. Both are priced in U.S. dollars, and both focus on low-sulfur grades of crude oil known as *sweet*.

Oil benchmarks are what their name implies. They set reference prices for crude oil, doing so through futures contracts that set oil prices for future months. The contracts serve as a useful hedge both for oil buyers—the refiners—and for oil producers against sudden spikes or drops in oil's price.

When a buyer contracts to buy oil from a producer, there's generally a significant time lag between the date the purchase was agreed to and the date the oil actually is delivered. Buyers want assurance that they won't end up paying far more than they expected if oil prices spike in the interim. Similarly, sellers want to know that they won't lose out should oil prices drop.

The futures contracts also are grist for speculators who have no intention of ever taking possession of oil but who make bets on whether oil prices will move higher or lower than the contract price. If they're right—say if they've bet on higher prices and prices do move past the contract price—they can buy at the contract price and immediately sell at the higher price for a quick profit.

There are obvious reasons China wants to challenge the long-time dominance of Brent and WTI with an Eastern yuan-based benchmark. After all, as indicated earlier, China already has established itself as right in the thick of oil markets. It imports the most oil, stockpiles the most oil, and is on track to refine the most oil. In addition, it focuses on different grades of oil from those priced by the Western benchmarks, preferring grades known as *medium sour*. And yet China's oil transactions are still priced in dollars based on prices set by Brent and WTI.

China's yuan-denominated oil benchmark is hosted by the Shanghai International Energy Exchange (INE), which is located within the Shanghai free-trade zone. China's free-trade zones—the Shanghai zone, established in 2013, was the first in what are now 12 zones—are free of most of the restrictions that can bedevil commerce elsewhere in China. Among other advantages, manufacturing, importing, and exporting can take place without intervention by customs authorities, helping attract foreign companies and investors.

After the benchmark's March 2018 launch, futures trading in the contract picked up steam. At times trading volume has been nearly equal to trading in one of the world's two major contracts, Brent. Still, a large amount of the trading is both domestic and speculative (traders looking for short-term gains rather than buying or selling with intent of actually taking possession of or delivering oil). It's an open question whether the contract will attract enough volume and international participation to pose a real threat to the dominance of Brent and WTI.

Not surprisingly, analysts disagree on the answer. Some say that it's not likely, or won't happen for a very long time. Others think that the Eastern benchmark ultimately could take significant share away from the Western benchmarks, making China a competing global oil trading center and leading to greater international acceptance of the yuan. But there's wide agreement that for foreigners to feel confident about investing in China and accepting payments in yuan, China first needs to take additional giant steps to liberalize its economy—to make it more open and transparent and the yuan less subject to government intervention.

This is a valid point. It's one that China understands as well as anyone. China has made clear that it plans, if cautiously, to do what it takes to bring the benchmark to the next level. Remember, China plays the long game. It didn't enter into its oil benchmark hastily or on a whim. It is an important part of its overall vision for its future, which makes the odds that it will succeed very high.

As the benchmark continues to gain traction, it will make the yuan much easier to use to price and trade oil within a significant part of the world, starting with the vast area encompassing Belt and Road Initiative (BRI) countries. This would be an important initial step in eroding the dollar's dominance in international trade and in shifting to a new monetary reserve system that will cover trade in more than oil and other commodities.

Worth noting, too, is that China already has entered into bilateral trade agreements in which it conducts trade in yuan, including with Russia, Iran, and Pakistan. Among other advantages, paying for oil imports with yuan allows China to continue to purchase oil from countries the United States has imposed sanctions on, such as Iran and Venezuela.

The Gold Factor

There's something else to know about the Eastern oil benchmark, something that I see as extremely significant but that has gotten little attention. It's the link between the yuan-denominated benchmark and gold.

In the summer of 2016, in an article I wrote for the website King World News, I said that China was getting closer to establishing a yuan-denominated oil benchmark. I further predicted that yuan used in trading oil would be backed by gold, enhancing its credibility and appeal.

The following year, my prediction was echoed in the publication *Asian Review*. It ran an article asserting that China's preparations for a yuan-denominated benchmark were proceeding apace and added that the yuan would be backed by gold. Only a few financial outlets in the West picked up the story, and the report did not make waves here.

The benchmark's launch itself, in March 2018, did get attention in the financial media and in oil industry publications. It generally was seen as part of China's effort to internationalize the yuan. The consensus was that it would take a long time for the new benchmark to have much of an impact on oil markets or the dollar. No one that I am aware of mentioned a connection to gold.

What is that connection? As I mentioned earlier, the benchmark is domiciled within the Shanghai free-trade zone. That zone also is home to the Shanghai Gold Exchange, a market where gold can be freely traded by foreigners. In China, gold trades are almost always settled with the exchange of actual physical gold. Indeed, China's gold exchange is the largest in the world for trading physical gold. Western trading in gold, by contrast, is like Chinese trading in oil: it's largely speculative, with little gold actually changing hands.

Also significant: while in most of China it's forbidden to take gold out of the country, that restriction does not apply within the free-trade zone. Foreigners who exchange yuan for gold in the free-trade zone can take the gold wherever they wish.

The ability to exchange yuan for gold in the context of the new Eastern oil benchmark is significant. It provides a foretaste of China's plan for a new monetary system in which gold is linked to fiat currencies. It's a smaller-scale step in which China's larger ambitions can be perceived.

In allowing the yuan to be traded for gold, China is making a statement: *the yuan is as good as gold.* This carries weight because from a long-term perspective, gold has maintained its value far better than the dollar has. Between the mid-1920s and the present, the dollar has lost about 95 percent of its value. Over the same period, gold has appreciated more than fourfold. If China can establish the yuan as being as good as gold, it's a powerful incentive for traders in oil (and other commodities as well) to accept the yuan. This, in turn, is an initial step toward creation of a new reserve currency unit that includes the yuan in a basket with many other currencies and that is backed by gold, China's ultimate aim.

A Striking Relationship

In this connection, another anomaly caught my eye in the months prior to the launch of the Eastern benchmark. Like the benchmark's link to gold, it went largely unnoticed. It had to do with how gold was being priced.

If you were an investor in 2018, you likely still have painful memories of how unnervingly volatile the financial markets were that year. U.S. stock markets experienced two deep corrections. The first occurred early in the year and was brief but vicious. From its high of 2,875 on January 29, the Standard and Poor's 500 Index (S&P 500) plunged within two weeks to 2,533, a 12 percent correction that seemingly came out of the blue.

The markets then recovered, and by September 21, the S&P 500 traded as high as 2,941. It seemed that all was well and that the year would end up being another win for investors, especially given that November, December, and January typically are seasonally strong months. Despite the February correction, the market seemed poised for double-digit gains in 2018.

Then came November and, even more harrowing, December. By December 26, the market traded as low as 2,347. This drop of 20 percent skirted being deemed a full-fledged bear market only because the high and low numbers were based on intraday, not closing, lows. The drop more than wiped out the entire year's gains.

The vertiginous swoops in the Dow Jones Industrial Average, which for many investors is synonymous with the market, perhaps struck investors as even more sickening. As October 2018 began, the Dow was near 26,800. On October 3, it hit its high point for the year, just above 26,950.

Then the rout began. By October 12, the Dow had dropped 1,800 points, closing a bit above 25,000—a nearly 2,000-point drop in seven trading days, more than 250 points a day on average.

It then began to recover, and on December 3, the Dow hit 25,980. Then another plunge: within four days it was trading below 23,900, an average drop of 500 points a day. It continued to fall, reaching its low of 22,686 on January 4, 2019. Then it abruptly turned around and began to march upward, getting back to 26,000 territory by late March.

Clearly, whatever words you choose to characterize the action of stock markets in 2018 and the first quarter of 2019, they aren't likely to include *calm*, *steady*, or *predictable*. Other assets during that stretch were volatile as well—even traditional safe havens such as Treasury bills were very volatile.

But there was one striking exception, an asset that displayed almost no volatility. That asset was gold—gold, that is, priced in yuan—in other words, gold that was traded on the Chinese gold exchange.

As I followed gold's course during 2018, it jumped out at me how consistently the yuan and gold were tracking each other. At the end of January, an ounce of gold was priced at around 8,500 yuan. As 2018 proceeded, gold's monthly closing low was 8,200 yuan in September, while the high, reached on the last day of December 2018, was 8,800 yuan. From top to bottom, this represented a range of 7 percent in monthly closing prices.

Moreover, I realized that the relationship extended as far back as March 2017. Indeed, if you took 12-month averages of the monthly closing price of gold, there was virtually no volatility at all for more than two years, through April 2019. Specifically, the range between high and low over more than two years was less than 2 percent.

Gold priced in dollars, while less volatile than stocks, was far less consistent than gold priced in yuan. Monthly closing prices ranged from a low of $1,184 an ounce to a high of $1,350, a 12 percent difference—around 64 percent more volatile than gold priced in yuan. If you used average monthly closes, the volatility of dollar-priced gold was nearly three times greater than that of yuan-priced gold.

The relationship between the yuan and gold was too consistent to be a coincidence. My best guess is that China engineered it with the intent of making the compelling point that the yuan is as good as gold. Regardless, the relationship between the yuan and gold over that time period is certainly thought provoking.

If the explanation for the relationship between the yuan and the price of gold is speculative, what's not speculative is China's ambition to make its oil benchmark a player in the global oil market. Assuring traders that they are paying for oil in a currency as good as gold is a great starting point toward reaching that goal. And it's also a clear indication of the importance China places on bringing gold into its monetary plans.

12

A New Reserve Currency, Part 1

WHO, WHEN, WHERE, what, and why? As aspiring journalists have long been taught, these questions should be answered in every story they write. In predicting a new monetary reserve system that will propel gold to new heights, I should answer them as well.

The "who" is China. The "when" is sometime in the not too distant future. The "where" is at the very least in the East and possibly beyond. The "why" is China's determination to get out from under the tyranny of the dollar and put in place a system that will avoid any replay of the catastrophe that unfolded in 2008.

This leaves the "what." If China were simply looking to replace the dollar with the yuan, it would be simple to describe. But this is not what China wants. Its thinking is more nuanced, as Zhou Xiaochuan made plain in his 2009 essay invoking the Triffin dilemma to explain why no sovereign currency should serve as the reserve currency. I've described China's goal as "a basket of currencies linked to gold." (The dollar would likely be one of those currencies but no longer the primary reserve currency.) This is a convenient thumbnail summary. But it leaves a lot to flesh out.

I take a stab at doing so here and in Chapter 13. Be forewarned, however, that my comments should be viewed as very largely speculative. China has provided strong hints about what it wants, and intriguing signposts have emerged, but there's no hard and fast blueprint. I do expect that the broad strokes I lay out will be on target. But the details could vary considerably. In fact, China itself likely hasn't worked out every detail and will adjust as needed to changing world dynamics.

First, a quick review of what a reserve currency does. It makes it possible for countries, each with its own sovereign currency, to trade with each other. If people, companies, and governments purchased only things made inside their own countries' borders, a reserve currency wouldn't be needed. But this isn't how the world works: Everyone in today's world wants to buy from and sell to countries around the globe.

If there were no reserve currency and, say, a Mexican restaurant chain wanted to buy stoves from a German company, which was thrilled to sell its stoves to Mexico, how would the companies handle the purchase? There'd be no easy way. The Germans would have no use for Mexican pesos, and the Mexicans wouldn't have the euros to buy the stoves. Any attempt to work out a solution that involved some sort of barter would be exceedingly clumsy and inefficient.

Enter the dollar. As the reserve currency, the dollar is accepted everywhere, with little or no fuss. It's readily converted into the native currency of every major economy. In Europe, it's accepted in lieu of the euro. And if your credit card is serviced by a dollar-based bank, you can charge purchases on your card, with currency conversations made automatically. Central banks in every country hold dollars as foreign reserves, and as long as enough dollars are spread around to provide the system with sufficient liquidity, the wheels of international trade can turn.

At times, the dollar has needed help in carrying out its role of providing liquidity. This is why in 1969 the International Monetary Fund (IMF) created monetary units known as *special drawing rights* (SDRs), designed to serve as a monetary reserve supplement. Each SDR unit represents a basket of five currencies, including the dollar, the pound sterling, the yen, the euro, and, since 2016, the yuan. Central banks can hold SDRs as a supplement to the dollar, and governments—but only governments, not individuals or businesses—can use SDRs for international financial transactions. The SDRs are managed by the IMF and guaranteed by the countries whose currencies comprise them.

The SDR never made much of a dent, however. For one thing, the total value of SDRs issued so far amounts to about $290 billion, far too little to be meaningful as a reserve currency. SDRs helped out in the 2008 financial crisis, but by and large, their role has been limited.

As currently constituted, any attempt to expand the role of SDRs in global monetary transactions would run into immediate difficulties. You don't have to be a hard money person to see why. For one thing, SDRs can be created out of thin air. The IMF can print as many as it pleases, increasing the worldwide money supply on a whim. The recent selection of an IMF chief engendered bitter squabbling among the Europeans, who by tradition select the person to occupy that position. That spat would be mild compared with the disputes that would erupt if the organization suddenly gained decisive power over trade flows.

Moreover, the individual countries whose currencies constitute the SDR, regardless of how low their weightings in it are, could print enough money to buy as many SDRs as they want. A country with just a 1 percent weighting could go wild printing 100-unit notes. You could enact rules against flagrant money printing, but who would be the rule keeper?

These are some of the drawbacks of the existing SDR that a future basket of currencies will need to overcome.

Still, the SDR serves as a kind of initial rough prototype, a starting point, for what China has in mind—with some extremely significant differences. The ultimate version, which could be dubbed anything but which for now I'll refer to as the *new SDR*, will be more expansive, more sophisticated in how it is calculated, digitized, more widely used, and—most important of all, raising it to an entirely different plane—it will be linked to gold.

A Digital Currency

One difference between the old and the new SDR is that the latter will be comprised of a much bigger assortment of currencies. Like the existing SDR, it will include the yuan, the dollar, the euro, the yen, and the British pound. But joining these will be other currencies, possibly the ruble, the rupee, the Mexican peso, and more. Each currency will be assigned a relative weighting based on the size of the gross domestic product of the country that issues it or a related metric. This, along with currency fluctuations, will determine how many SDRs a particular currency can buy. When a currency is rising relative to others, it will be worth more SDRs than when it is falling.

A second and more striking difference is that the new SDR will be digital—it will be a *cryptocurrency*. A digitized currency based on the technology known as *blockchain* would have enormous advantages. Transactions could be recorded instantaneously and distributed to any number of relevant parties. A blockchain would create a permanent record of all international transactions and would be much more efficient than today's clearing mechanisms. It would be easy for the IMF, or whatever entity was put in charge of the new system, to monitor and manage it.

The most complicated aspect of the new SDR, with its collection of differentially weighted currencies, would be establishing a trading system. This is where blockchain would really show its chops. These units of information could surmount all the problems associated with the transfer of funds, including identification of the transferee, the possibility of hacking, and the need for a paper trail.

China happens—and, no surprise, it's not happenstance—to be particularly well positioned to take charge of shepherding a new digital currency into existence and establishing the parameters of the associated blockchain. It has been preparing for years.

Both blockchains and cryptocurrencies are created by incredibly complex software and require highly advanced technical skills. China has made sure that it is rich in talent in this area. A few years back, it banned all trading of cryptocurrencies in China, but it did not ban the *mining* of cryptocurrencies. Quite the opposite. It was and remains the world's biggest miner of cryptocurrencies, leading to an abundance of expertise on which it will be able to draw.

In mining cryptocurrencies, China has been helped by another kind of abundance, its hydropower resources. They provide essentially free energy, a huge plus when it comes to running the enormously complicated and energy-intensive algorithms required for cryptocurrency mining.

China's outsized role in creation of the new SDR won't mean that China can cheat. Once a cryptocurrency and associated blockchain ledger are created, they are impenetrable.

A digitized SDR offers many advantages. Still, on its own, digitization doesn't address all the drawbacks I noted earlier of the existing SDR. Notably, it wouldn't curb the potential for monetary inflation. Nor would it eliminate the dollar as the de facto reserve currency.

This is because nothing would prevent competing cryptocurrencies from being created. Recently, for instance, Facebook announced plans for its own cryptocurrency, Libra. As summarized in the *South China Morning Post* in an article on July 2, 2019, Libra will be linked to a basket of major currencies and governed by a Switzerland-based non-profit consortium, the Libra Association, which includes more than two dozen companies, including Visa, Mastercard, PayPal, Stripe, eBay, Uber.

Wang Xin, head of research for the People's Bank of China, points to why China wouldn't support an alternate currency like Libra. On July 8, 2019, addressing a conference hosted by Peking University's Institute of Digital Finance, he said that if Libra is closely associated with the U.S. dollar "it could create a scenario under which sovereign currencies would coexist with U.S. dollar–centric digital currencies. But there would be in essence one boss, that is, the U.S. dollar and the United States. If so, it would bring a series of economic, financial and even international political consequences." This is exactly what China wants to avoid.

Digitization of the new SDR would take China partway to its goal. But one more piece is still needed. That piece is gold. Bringing in gold would completely rewrite the rules of the game. Backed by gold, the SDR would have the credibility to gain widespread acceptance and rise above any competing currency, including the dollar. Lacking this link, it will likely fall flat, failing to win acceptance even within the Eastern and developing world, much less on a global scale.

The gold–SDR tie—which will be entirely different from the old gold standard—is so important, and so complex, and has so many ramifications and is so central to the case for an unparalleled bull market in gold that I am not going to cover it here. As with an inset in a map, it requires being looked at on its own, in a separate chapter, which follows this one. Before getting to it, I have a few more comments that bear on China's ability to pull a new SDR off.

Getting from Here to There

Besides the "what," there's actually another question I need to answer, one that doesn't start with a "w." It's "how." How does China get to a new monetary system? What must happen before the new SDR can become a reality? As I write this, many of the pieces have been put into place. Here are some thoughts on how the process might proceed.

I expect that Saudi Arabia will play a big part. Its long-standing commitment to price oil in dollars in exchange for U.S. military protection has been key in keeping the dollar as the reserve currency. This link between oil and the dollar remains strong. But it's not impregnable. China can chip away at it from two different directions.

One relates to the Eastern oil benchmark and its pricing of oil in yuan exchangeable for gold. I don't expect that the Chinese benchmark will serve as a significant conduit for the physical exchange of large amounts of oil. Rather, like other benchmarks, its primary role will be to set what the market considers to be fair prices. It already is playing such a role in price discovery.

Today, virtually all Saudi oil sold to China is through contracts that specify payment in dollars. But the Eastern benchmark is important because the dollars relate to yuan–dollar exchange rates, meaning that the price of oil in yuan is significant. It's relevant, too, that Saudi Arabia and Russia—by a wide margin the two largest Eastern suppliers of oil—produce relatively similar grades of oil. Russia generally prefers to get dollars, which its banks find more convenient to deal with. But it still has been willing to accept yuan on large oil contracts. This could give Russia an edge in terms of access to China's market that—all else equal—the Saudis would want to match by accommodating China's wish to have oil priced in yuan.

The bottom line is that I expect that there will be greater pricing of oil in yuan. The logical next move will come when Saudi contracts stop specifying the dollar, naming instead the yuan or a new SDR.

Dramatically loosening the tie between Saudi oil and the dollar would be a big step forward for China. But this is just one of the arrows in China's quiver—a metaphor that is particularly apt because a second line of attack could target the Saudis' military reliance on the United States. It's not far-fetched at all to think that China, which has far more than arrows in its military arsenal, can convince the Saudis that it can protect them better than the United States can.

The implicit premise underlying the U.S.–Saudi petrodollar deal, a pact made essentially on a handshake basis and not an actual treaty, was that the United States was the world's undisputed military hegemon. But China's military capabilities have been rapidly expanding and now rival or even surpass ours in some important ways, particularly when it comes to defensive systems.

Among other things, China (as has Russia) has developed hypersonic missiles that can fly at five or more times the speed of sound and are exceedingly difficult to detect or counter. They have the potential, without a nuclear payload, to sink an aircraft carrier. A recent report commissioned by the U.S. Air Force noted that when it comes to such technology, the U.S. "absence of a clear acquisition pathway . . . stands in stark contrast to potential adversaries' feverish pace of research and development. . . . Their investments have been significant . . . and their accomplishments in some cases startling." (The report commissioned by the U.S. Air Force was titled "Vigilance, Reach and Power:

High-Speed Maneuvering Weapons, Unclassified Summary," March 3, 2018.)

China recently showed off its newest stealth plane, the J-20, whose range is somewhat limited but whose maneuverability within its range is extraordinary. Similarly, in the realm of underwater protection, China has showcased its new stealth submarine. While its exact specs remain secret, it's clear from the design that the new underwater vessel is a quantum jump from earlier models. It's undetectable and capable of firing vertical missiles at any unwanted intruder.

The point is that while by most widely used measures the West's military is mightier, China has a military better designed for meeting certain basic needs of protection and security in today's world, especially when you include cybersecurity.

The out-of-the-blue attack in September 2019 that crippled important parts of Saudi Arabia's oil infrastructure no doubt made a deep impression on the Saudis and clearly exposed their vulnerabilities. For the Saudis, continued reliance on the United States as their main protector in preference to closer military ties to China as well as Russia, which also is eager to see the dollar replaced as the world's reserve currency, might come to seem a dubious choice.

I could go on about the military implications. For instance, I could note that not just Saudi Arabia but other Gulf States as well might accept China as their main protector. Or more likely, they might rely on a combination of China and Russia, which have been working together since the mid-1990s to establish a security sphere that encompasses Eurasia and more. The Shanghai Cooperation Organization (SCO) was originally set up as a security and economic organization for China, Russia, and four Central Asian countries. In 2017, it was broadened to include archenemies Pakistan and India, which says worlds about China's influence in the East.

And the latest development as I write this, the U.S. retreat in Syria and abandonment of the Kurds can only make other countries further question relying on the United States to protect them and look for alternatives, one more example of the United States creating a vacuum begging to be filled.

But I want to turn my attention back to the most important feature of the new SDR and the one most directly relevant to gold investors: its backing by gold. This is at the heart of the case for a powerful rise in gold prices in coming years.

13
A New Reserve Currency, Part 2

GOLD WILL BACK a new reserve currency, pushing gold prices far higher. Of that much I'm certain.

But the precise form the new system will take and the precise way gold will be brought in—and what it will mean for gold's ultimate price—will become clear only over time. I can speculate about it here, but I freely admit that *speculate* is the operative word.

In this chapter, I offer some ideas that seem plausible to me for how it all will shape up. Clearly, if I'm at all on target, in the coming years, the world's monetary relationships will look radically different from today. And clearly, the price of gold will be far, far higher.

Before diving in, I'll emphasize again that this will be nothing like your grandfather's gold standard, where gold was fixed in price relative to paper currencies. In the old days, under the old gold standard, a fixed rate was feasible because the amount of gold mined each year kept rough pace with economic growth from expanding populations and productivity gains.

Today, though, we are near peak gold. Although gold still is being mined, growth in production has begun to slow sharply, and the cost of production has been increasing. For the foreseeable future, the amount of gold above ground will dwarf potential gold reserves underground. Under these circumstances, tethering a currency to gold at a fixed rate would be disastrously deflationary, potentially putting a stranglehold on global economic growth. The new gold standard will be a whole new animal: a gold-backed currency that lets gold rise to accommodate expanding economic activity, especially growing international trade.

Fixed Amounts of Gold

In Chapter 3, I described gold's many special qualities that have made it prized over the centuries. Here I'll note just one that's particularly relevant to gold's role in a reserve currency: unlike other metals, which have extensive industrial uses and therefore get used up, the amount of gold in the world is relatively fixed.

Only about 10 percent of gold that is produced goes to industry, and those applications have readily available substitutes. Moreover, because gold is relatively indestructible, even gold put to industrial use can be recycled. Gold's main use is as a store of value, whether in the form of bars, coins, or jewelry. The World Gold Council believes that virtually all the gold that has ever been mined remains part of the world's inventory.

How much gold is this? Estimates of above-ground gold range from around 175,000 to 195,000 metric tons. Below-ground reserves, according to the United States Geological Survey, are about 54,000 metric tons.

As gold prices rise, so will estimates of below-ground reserves. But sharply rising mining costs will mean that there's a significant discount between above- and below-ground gold.

Jewelry accounts for about half the above-ground gold, or a bit above 90,000 metric tons. Reported gold holdings of central banks are a bit above 34,000 metric tons. Use in industry accounts for a little less than 20,000 metric tons. The remainder is dedicated to private investments such as coins and bars stored in vaults and gold exchange-traded funds (ETFs).

Most analysts who expect that gold will play a monetary role focus on central bank holdings. But I think that even jewelry will start to come into play as higher gold prices tempt people to sell their gold necklaces and bracelets.

These ballpark estimates of the amount of gold in the world are the starting point for tackling all the other relevant questions about gold's future monetary role and price.

The Bank of International Settlements and Bank Balance Sheets

In assessing the various forces that will combine to elevate gold's monetary role, one topic I need to revisit is a recent action by the Bank of International Settlements (BIS), an international entity often called the *central bank for central banks*. One of BIS's responsibilities is to periodically make recommendations relating to the risk ratios banks should maintain. This became particularly urgent after the 2008 financial debacle, which occurred because many banks held, as assets, loans that turned out to be worthless, sparking bank runs that threatened to topple the whole system.

In the aftermath of the 2008 financial crisis, BIS indeed issued new guidelines. Inexplicably, though, these guidelines failed to include gold as a riskless asset. What makes this omission so surprising is that during the crisis, gold not only provided a vital hedge and was the best source of liquidity among all major assets, but its volatility during the financial crisis was relatively low. As I noted in Chapter 2, the BIS guidelines seemed to be evidence of a deliberate bias against acknowledging gold as a monetary metal.

Since then, BIS has been working on a new set of recommendations. And now BIS seems on board to elevate gold's role on bank balance sheets.

Not that it trumpeted this change in bold headlines. BIS is not known for flamboyance. The critical line appears on page 32 of a 162-page December 2017 white paper. I cited it in Chapter 2, but I'll repeat it here. It reads: "A 0% risk weight will apply to (i) cash owned and held at the bank or in transit; and (ii) gold bullion held at the bank or held in another bank on an allocated basis to the extent the gold bullion assets are backed by gold bullion liabilities."

That recommendation took effect in March 2019. If it strikes you as opaque, you're right. I'll try to deconstruct what it authorizes and why it's significant.

A bank, like any other company, carries assets and liabilities on its balance sheet. Bank assets include loans, bonds, equities, cash, and gold. In calculating how safe or risky a bank is, BIS assigns assets degrees of risk, with some assets viewed as having zero risk. These include cash, and since March 2019, they also include some gold.

Unlike assets that pre-2008 had been deemed low risk and then failed—not so low risk after all—gold and cash can't fail. However, gold can fluctuate in value, which from a shorter-term perspective can be viewed as a risk. In the past half century, gold has swung from about $35 an ounce to $800 to $250 and, as of this writing, to $1,500. These are big swings, with many fluctuations in between.

On the positive side, gold has no counterparty. If a bank holds gold, the bank does not depend on someone else paying it back, someone who might for one reason or another decide to skip town. And longer-term history is on gold's side relative to the dollar or any other paper currency. During the 50 years in which gold went from $35 to $1,500, the dollar's purchasing power relative to gold went from a dollar purchasing one-thirty-fifth of an ounce to its purchasing today of one-fifteen-hundredth of an ounce.

Still, it would be nice to be able to count on some consistency over the shorter term as well. An ultrasafe monetary policy should leave nothing to chance. And it turns out that in holding gold, banks are less vulnerable to its shorter-term fluctuations than it might initially appear.

Let's return to a bank's balance sheet. The left-hand side shows assets. The right-hand side shows debts along with the bank's equity, which is the difference between assets and debts.

For a bank, deposits are the most important component of debt. When bank customers deposit money into their checking or savings accounts, it's an asset for the customers. But for the bank, it counts as debt—it's money the bank owes to depositors.

The BIS sentence I cited earlier refers to "gold liabilities." The term may strike most Westerners as puzzling, but Easterners would readily grasp it. Gold liabilities are simply deposits—savings deposits, demand deposits, or any variation—denominated not in cash but in gold. These are common in Eastern banks.

This gives Eastern banks that hold gold as an asset a nifty buffer against dips in gold's price. If the gold price goes down, the value of the gold the banks hold as an asset will drop as well. But counteracting that, the banks' gold liabilities will simultaneously decrease as well. To the extent that gold assets are offset by gold deposits, the banks won't suffer if the price of gold falls and won't need to pony up additional assets to maintain a steady risk ratio. These relationships explain BIS's language, in which gold is considered riskless only insofar as gold assets are offset by gold liabilities.

You still could argue that there are risks—for instance, trading losses on gold deposits could spark a run by depositors on their gold deposits. But there are ways to protect against this. A central bank could put a floor under gold, permitting it to drop only so far and no lower. In the past, gold has been barred from trading below various arbitrary levels, including $20 and $35.

In the new monetary system I'm speculating about, such a floor could be in the form of a band, that is, a trading range around a midpoint. It could be managed by a consortium of independent institutions such as the International Monetary Fund, BIS, and the World Bank, along with representatives from the world's largest economies. These institutions would control the gold that backs up the new SDR and would have the power to keep gold in a trading range that they would set.

And if depositors wanted to cash out when gold soars in price? One solution could be to set one price for cashing out to pocket a gain and a different, higher price for cashing out to afford, say, medical care. This would be entirely feasible. In fact, and here I'm really letting my imagination roam freely, this kind of flexibility someday may form the basis for administering entitlement programs that expand and improve a society's safety net.

Is There Enough Gold?

In speculating about a new gold-backed monetary system, a central question is how the world's store of gold matches up against the gold such a system would need. Answering this question goes to the heart of why I expect gold prices to soar.

Let's figure that above-ground gold amounts to 190,000 metric tons, slightly above the midpoint of the consensus estimates referenced earlier. Gold's current price of $1,460 an ounce amounts to around $51.60 per gram. This makes a metric ton of gold worth about $51.6 million. Multiplying this by 190,000, you get $8.9 trillion worth of gold in the world at the present moment.

This is a big number. But it's not nearly big enough for gold to do all that it will be called on to do in coming years. For gold to take on those jobs, its price will need to rise significantly.

Note that I said *jobs*, plural. Backing a new reserve currency that can ensure a more stable global system will be one of them. But I expect that there will be other related ones as well. Gold will come into play in helping the world deal with the huge amount of debt that permeates the global financial landscape. It will also play a role as the world is forced to spend vast sums chasing down dwindling resources, resources that are an essential bridge to a world less dependent on those finite resources.

As resource scarcities become more evident, gold will be seen as the asset best suited to mediating them. This role is one of the most powerful arguments for a gold-backed monetary system. Any currency backed by paper would fail as a pricing mechanism for scarce assets as countries race to print more paper.

China's continued accumulation of gold positions it to lead in crafting a new system that will address these challenges. How much gold does China have? I can offer only two answers with any certainty. One, it has a lot. And two, it has more than it is letting on. The rest is all guesswork and estimates. But the best guess is that China may have more gold than any other country in the world.

After all, China remains the largest miner of gold, mining around 400 tons a year despite its relatively paltry reserve base. It also imports a lot of gold, coming through Hong Kong and various Chinese ports. Since the beginning of the decade, Chinese production plus known imports from two places—Hong Kong and Switzerland—have averaged about 1,500 metric tons a year. And China obtains gold from various other countries as well.

On top of this is gold imported by China's central bank, the People's Bank of China (PBOC). This monetary gold occupies a special status and does not have to be reported, making it particularly opaque. The official PBOC figure for its gold holdings is about 2,000 metric tons, but this is likely significantly understated. Most analysts, including Bloomberg, believe that the actual figure is at least 3,000 and possibly a lot higher.

Then you need to include the gold in China before the decade started. A final factor is that almost all the gold in China stays in China. Remember, it's forbidden to export gold from China other than from free-trade zones. Exports from those zones are known to be de minimis.

What does this all add up to? Most estimates of Chinese gold usually start at about 20,000 metric tons and run as high as more than 30,000 metric tons. Gold seller Singapore-based Bullion Star probably has done the most careful work on the subject. It estimates, and it acknowledges that this is just an estimate, that China has around 25,000 metric tons.

Based on my calculations, a total of 25,000 metric tons, and even 30,000 metric tons, rings true.

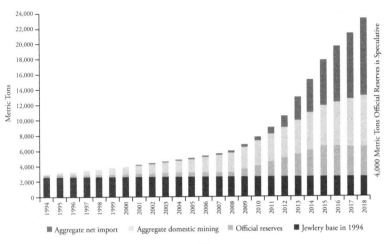

FIGURE 13.1   Estimated total Chinese gold reserves.
Source: BullionStar.com.

China's Advantage

An important question is how much of that gold ends up in commercial banks. The World Gold Council estimates that about 55 percent of China's gold finds its way into the hands of the public. Commercial banks hold a fair amount of that and—unlike Western banks—carry both gold assets and liabilities on their balance sheets.

Under the new BIS guidelines defining the circumstances that make gold a riskless asset, China has a distinct advantage. This is because over the past decade—and this likely qualifies as an example of its long-term thinking—the Chinese government has urged Chinese citizens to accumulate gold. As part of this campaign, banks have instituted and aggressively promoted various gold-accumulation plans (GAPs). These plans resemble the automatic stock-accumulation plans Western financial planners often recommend, which allow investors to accumulate stocks on a steady, measured basis without worrying about timing the market. The idea is that each month, whatever the market has done, you buy a set number of shares. As long as the market is in a long-term uptrend and you stick with the plan long enough, the plan guarantees gains.

In China, banks buy gold, whether from the central bank, the physical gold exchange, a mining company, or some other source, and then each month sell a fixed amount to their GAP customers. And presto, banks have continually rising liabilities to offset their gold assets. GAPs are just one way a bank can create gold liabilities. Storing gold for customers also works because it creates a gold deposit "allocated" to a customer, which the bank, if need be, can offset by buying gold on the open market.

In 2018, right after the new BIS regulations were released, the world's central banks began buying gold hand over fist. I don't think that this is a coincidence. Not all commercial banks have ready sources from which they can buy physical gold. If banks in the West tried to accumulate physical gold through the futures markets, it would create a massive squeeze because the system doesn't have enough gold to satisfy such demand. Instead, futures are closed out for cash at expiration. By contrast, futures traded on the Shanghai futures exchange are almost always settled with gold exchanging hands.

Through its holdings of gold in both the PBOC and commercial banks, China has a major edge in a monetary gold-centered system. But the West could still participate, with the gold that Western central banks have started accumulating then coming into play. That gold could serve both as a source of gold assets—when commercial banks buy gold from a central bank—and as a source of liabilities if the central bank stores gold at a commercial bank. With central banks relatively free to do business among themselves, commercial banks throughout the West would have a growing source of gold assets and liabilities.

I'm speculating that the gold held by central banks likely would back up international trade, whereas the gold held by commercial banks would back up domestic transactions. The beauty of such a monetary system would be that the rising gold prices needed for gold to back international trade, and perhaps domestic transactions within countries as well, automatically would strengthen commercial banks throughout the world. In other words, this pathway to bringing gold into a new monetary system could make the world much healthier financially, inoculated for a long time to come against the kind of crisis that traumatized the world in 2008.

Envisioning the New System

When might all this happen? What will galvanize it? How will the process develop? Again, I'm happy to speculate.

My guess is that the system will start to take shape as China gains somewhat more power over the pricing of oil. This will likely happen once Saudi oil contracts no longer specify payment in dollars, as I discussed in Chapter 12. This could help win the support of some Eastern developing countries and perhaps some European countries as well for a new currency unit for conducting international trade.

Some countries might be motivated by a desire to elude U.S. sanctions power. But the United States itself might end up joining in the new currency to ensure that the dollar continues to play a role in world trade, with the U.S. Federal Reserve looking to add gold to its holdings so as to strengthen U.S. commercial banks.

Currencies participating in the new SDR would be assigned a weighting in the unit based on a metric such as gross domestic product (GDP) or the percentage of international trade it accounts for. One question will be whether units of trade are based on dollars or, what perhaps is likelier, on purchasing power parity (PPP).

Each country will be expected to have on hand an amount of gold that corresponds in some way to its share of the new SDR. A country with insufficient gold holdings could borrow gold and pay it back over time. China no doubt would willingly lend gold to some of its Eastern trading partners to allow them to participate in the new SDR. In the aggregate, all this gold will provide backing for the new unit.

The new SDR would be administered and monitored by the kind of independent consortium of respected international bodies I referred to earlier, likely including the IMF, BIS, and the World Bank, perhaps with representatives from the individual countries. The administering body would issue regulations and have the power to set gold's price.

It might operate somewhat as the Federal Reserve does or, more accurately, as it used to. When I started out in this business, the Fed did everything in secret. It didn't announce a decision to raise or lower interest rates, as it does today. The public learned about a change in Fed policy only when the Fed entered the fed funds market to buy or sell.

For instance, if the fed funds rate (the prevailing rate for bank-to-bank loans and the rate the Fed directly controls through open-market operations) were 5 percent, and the Fed went in and bought fed funds, it would signal looser monetary policy. If the Fed sold, it would mean the reverse. For the entity in charge of the new SDR, operating in a comparable manner might help it to effect changes in gold more gradually, avoiding big dramatic swings. Just as the Fed's massive holdings of dollars allowed it to control the fed funds rate, the new entity's effective holdings of gold will give it control.

Clearly, the system I'm describing would be enormously complex. After all, it involves tracking every single international transaction. This could be done only through blockchain technology. A blockchain, a distributed database that can reach a mind-boggling level of complexity, could ensure a permanent record of all nation-to-nation trades and allow the system to function smoothly.

China, thanks to all the gold it has accumulated and its leading position in blockchain technology, has positioned itself to help breathe life into the new SDR. Moreover, I wouldn't be surprised if China and other countries that have abundant gold eventually create two cryptocurrencies, both backed by gold. One, the new SDR, will be for international transactions. The other will be for domestic use. Backing a domestic cryptocurrency with gold would ensure that countries properly manage their sovereign currencies. There could be penalties for countries whose money supply grows faster than nominal GDP.

How High Can Gold Go?

At the end of the day, for investors, only one thing counts: how high will gold go? What will all these changes in monetary relationships mean for gold's future price? Again, I'm happy to speculate.

I noted earlier that gold's present value of $8.9 trillion isn't nearly enough to back the new SDR. So I'll start by calculating—speculating—how high gold would need to go simply to carry out this one major job. The following figures seem plausible to me.

The gold that's immediately available for worldwide monetary use, meaning parked in central banks, amounts to about 32,000 metric tons. At today's price of $1,460 an ounce or $51.60 per gram, this would provide about $1.5 trillion to back international trade. This is a far cry from the total amount of the world's imports (or exports) today, which amount to about $25 trillion. To provide backing for all international trade, gold would have to rise to about $24,000 per ounce (25/1.5 multiplied by $1,460). In other words, the gold price would have to rise more than 16-fold.

Now before you start dreaming of waking up one fine morning and finding that overnight your gold holdings have climbed by more than 16-fold, realize that the process will be gradual. Once oil is denominated in currencies other than the dollar, other commodities would have to follow and then goods and services. Somewhere along the line, the crypto-blockchain SDR would have to be created. And not all countries would join at first.

So the bad news for gold investors is that they will need a lot of patience. The good news is that gold's ultimate stopping point will likely be far higher than $24,000.

Why? Because gold, remember, in the scenarios I'm envisioning won't be used just to back the new SDR used in international trade. Eventually, it also will back domestic currencies. And that provides a whole new tailwind for gold.

Interestingly, Bloomberg's intelligence team looked at a similar question in mid-2015, asking how high gold would have to go simply to back the yuan. The study assumed that China would use 10,000 metric tons to back up its readily accessible money, known as M2. It concluded that gold would have to trade at *$65,000 an ounce*. (And the article ran in June, so I couldn't even assume that it was an April Fool's joke.)

How would the numbers pan out if not just the yuan but all the world's M2 were backed by gold, and we used a more realistic and expansive estimate for the amount of gold involved? Let's assume that 70 percent of all the world's gold went to this purpose, with PPP the metric used to measure money supply and GDP. Under these assumptions, the relationship between M2 and GDP suggests that M2 would be around $140–$150 trillion. And 70 percent of the world's above-ground gold would amount to about 130,000 metric tons. This points to the price of gold rising to above $35,000 an ounce to back countries' domestic transactions, assuming that all countries participate.

These are all dynamic numbers. On the one hand, more gold will be mined. On the other hand, resource scarcities will likely drive M2 ever higher. My guess is that the rise in M2 will be greater than the value of the additional gold, meaning that $35,000 wouldn't be gold's stopping point.

Note that I'm *not* going to argue that the next step is to add $35,000 (the price of gold if it backs all domestic transactions) to $24,000 (gold's price from backing the new SDR) to arrive at a target price of $59,000 an ounce. This probably would be overshooting the mark, because there would be a degree of overlap between domestic and international transactions.

But don't let this disappoint you. If I'm at all correct in my assumptions and calculations, we are looking at what arguably will be the greatest bull market of all time. And with paper money likely to suffer in proportion to gold's gains, the consequences of missing out on this bull market won't just be a matter of letting an opportunity pass you by. The consequences could be financial devastation.

Can anything derail this scenario? In Chapter 14, I look at what the China bears most often cite as a potentially debilitating flaw that could bring China's economy down: China's debt.

14

How Bad Is China's Debt Problem?

STRATFOR IS AN American geopolitical intelligence company that publishes forecasts of global trends. In 2005, it confidently predicted that "China will suffer a meltdown like Japan and East and Southeast Asia before it. The staggering proportion of bad debt, enormous even in relation to official dollar reserves, represents a defining crisis for China." (Its report, China's Economy, Running on Borrowed Time," appeared on January 27, 2005.)

In 2010, hedge fund manager Jim Chanos, an oft-quoted darling of much of the financial media, said that China was on the verge of an economic collapse that would set it on a "treadmill to hell." And more recently, in February 2019, the *Financial Times* ran an article by Joseph Nye, a professor at Harvard's Kennedy School of Government, headlined, "China Will Not Surpass U.S. Anytime Soon." Nye dismissed purchasing power parity as a meaningful measure of influence and cited unnamed businesspeople who said that China's growth rate was likely less than half what China claimed. He concluded that it would take at least a decade or two before China overtakes the United States as the world's largest economy.

China's rise this century has been unprecedented in its scope and speed. And every step of the way, prominent voices in the West have insisted that China is about to fail. Time and again they've been wrong. Of course, this doesn't guarantee that the current batch of China skeptics will be wrong. Sometimes there really is a wolf.

Today, those who insist that China's economy is in trouble generally focus on China's high level of debt.

China's Overall Debt

Polonius famously and fatuously advised Hamlet "neither a borrower nor a lender be." Polonius, obviously, never would have made it in the modern capitalist world. Of course, he didn't fare so well in the sixteenth century either. Benjamin Franklin also took a dim view of debt, advising that it was better to "go to bed without dinner than to rise in debt."

A persistent knock against China has been that its economy is awash in bad debt, including huge amounts of hidden, or *shadow*, debt. China accumulated a lot of debt in the wake of the 2008 financial crisis, when, to keep growth going, local governments were required to spend heavily on new infrastructure projects. To do so, they borrowed huge amounts of money, funneled to them largely through corporate entities they created.

Some people estimate that total debt in China equals around 300 percent of gross domestic product (GDP). Others, including the Organisation for Economic Co-operation and Development (OECD), more optimistically put the number closer to 250 percent.

Either way, though, it is high—around twice what you'd expect for a developing country. It approaches levels of fully developed countries, which typically have higher amounts of debt because they can borrow more readily. Developed countries whose economies are trusted by investors can, without much trouble, support debt levels above 300 percent of GDP.

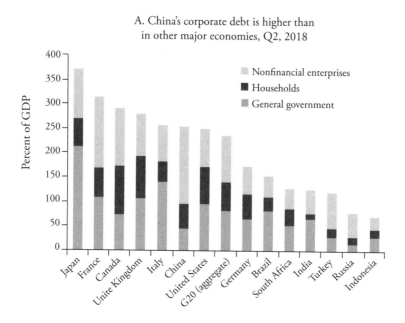

A. China's corporate debt is higher than in other major economies, Q2, 2018

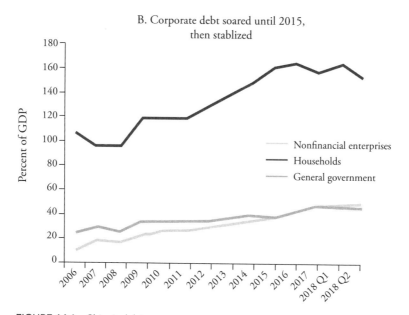

B. Corporate debt soared until 2015, then stablized

FIGURE 14.1   China's debt.

Source: Bank for International Settlements and OECD.

Under the worst-case scenario envisioned by today's China bears, high debt levels would drag China's economy into an abyss: companies would fail, banks would crater, and a growth slowdown would accelerate. Under such circumstances, it would be highly unlikely that China could prevail with a new monetary system. So it's worth trying to see just how big a problem China's debt really is.

That turned out to be no simple matter. China's debt has many components and moving parts. To get any handle on it required digging into a lot of numbers, some of which overlap in hard-to-decipher ways and at times seem contradictory. I had to make judgments as to which data and figures seemed most reliable and consistent. Here's my best stab at clarifying the overall picture.

Corporate Debt and State-Owned Enterprises

China's overall debt level is indisputably high. But only some of its components are worrisome. The greatest concern centers on corporate debt, estimated at around 170 percent of GDP. This is higher than for any other major economy.

Corporate debt itself has several different components. Again, while some are a problem, others are not. On the side of the not-a-problem corporate debt are around 4,000 private corporations. These are companies in which the government has no ownership stake, though they can be public companies in the sense that many are publicly traded on stock exchanges.

These companies are in good shape when it comes to debt, according to an extensive Bloomberg study released in late 2017. It looked at the ratio of debt to earnings (using the accounting measure earnings before interest, taxes, depreciation, and amortization [EBITDA]) and found that for the 4,000 private Chinese corporations (these excluded financial companies), the ratio was one. In other words, on average, the companies were taking in enough money to cover their debt, a clear sign that debt was not a problem.

When I came across the study, I was curious to know how the debt metrics Bloomberg presented for China's corporations compared with those for Standard and Poor's 500 Index (S&P 500) companies. So I plugged in the data and did the comparisons. The private Chinese companies, it turned out, were far *less* leveraged than the S&P 500 companies. For the latter, the ratio averaged 3.06 (on an unweighted basis) and only a bit better at 2.56 (on a weighted basis, where a company's capitalization is taken into account).

In other words, you really don't need to worry about debt on the books of China's private corporations. This, however, leaves a large group of other corporations to consider: China's state-owned enterprises (SOEs). In China, unlike the United States, the government owns or has a big share in numerous huge corporations, most of them operating in vital areas. These are the much-criticized SOEs.

Compared with the private corporations, SOEs are inefficient, as can be deduced from figures reported by the World Economic Forum. It found that private companies in China contribute around 60 percent of GDP, 70 percent of investment, and 80 percent of profits and employment while accounting for only about 30 percent of corporate debt. The SOEs, clearly, are far more leveraged than the private corporations, accounting for the remaining more than two-thirds of corporate debt in China.

But this is not as damning as it sounds, because SOEs, even if inefficient, aren't dead weight. Many perform vital functions that generate large amounts of revenue.

One example is China Petroleum and Chemical Corporation, also known as Sinopec, which trades on the New York Stock Exchange under the symbol SNP. This oil, gas, and chemical giant is the world's largest oil company. Its biggest division, refining, is a major exporter of gasoline and other refined oil and gas products. The company has a revenue stream in the hundreds of billions of dollars. This makes the fairly large amount of debt on its balance sheet manageable under almost any foreseeable circumstances.

Not all vital SOEs are publicly traded. One that is not is the State Grid Corporation of China, which manages most of China's power. Available information shows revenues of about $350 billion, up 20 percent in the most recent two years. The ratings agency Fitch Ratings gives the company's debt an A+ rating, several notches from the highest but still solid investment grade. The company is the world's largest utility and is assured of growth in China and in many Belt and Road Initiative (BRI) countries as well.

SOEs are overseen by an entity called the State-Owned Assets Supervision and Administration Commission (SASAC). Since 2008, SASAC has reduced the number of larger SOEs from more than 150 to about 100 today, largely through mergers and acquisitions among them. As a group, SOEs have impressive fundamentals. They have more than $26 trillion in assets, close to $25 trillion in revenue, and profits of about $500 billion, which reflects a low 2 percent return on assets. If combined, they would constitute, by a large margin, the world's largest company. They are massive and, on balance, profitable, and to borrow a useful term from Warren Buffett, they have deep franchises, meaning that they are shielded from competition.

None of this means that their high debt levels should be ignored. After all, debt is debt. Profits can turn into losses, and SOEs by and large have thin profit margins. An accelerating slowdown in global growth, whether from trade wars or other factors, could leave them exposed. For now, though, the debt levels carried by the majority of SOEs don't seem to be cause for alarm.

Zombies and Local Government Financing Vehicles

Once again, however, there are distinctions to be made. Some SOEs are in worse shape than the group overall, as you might surmise from their sobriquet *zombies*. The zombies, large industrial companies that produce steel, aluminum, cement, and paper, are plagued by overcapacity. To keep going, they must continually borrow more money.

China hasn't ignored their plight. Over the past few years, SASAC has worked to make zombies more efficient through mergers, the shuttering of excess capacity, and other steps. As of 2016, their debt had dropped to around 15 percent of total corporate debt, and it should drop further as more mergers take place.

The government had planned to eliminate the zombies entirely by 2020, but the trade wars could slow the process. Despite their losses, the zombies provide employment to a sizable number of workers. The government will be reluctant to shut them down until it is confident that economic growth will be strong enough to absorb their workers. Moreover, BRI countries may breathe new life into some zombies by using some of their excess capacity for infrastructure projects.

Even more troubling than zombie debt is debt in companies known as *local government financing vehicles* (LGFVs). Controlled by local or regional governments, they were created to finance the large infrastructure projects that localities launched as the 2008 global financial crisis worked its poisonous spell. They can be seen as a local analogue of the central-government-owned SOEs but with fewer advantages, because local governments have fewer resources and less leeway than the central government.

Regional governments resorted to creating LGFVs to get around the fact that local governments in China have limited sources of revenue. They can sell land, and they get a fixed share of taxes levied by the central government, but the central government limits how much they can borrow. The LGFVs let them skirt these limits. As corporate entities, LGFVs can issue bonds, get loans from banks that can be collateralized by regional assets and revenues, and even issue equity on the stock market or sell interests in their companies to institutional investors.

Not all LGFVs are problematic. But many are. And besides being debt heavy, they also are exceedingly opaque. In other words, it's hard to figure out exactly how bad off they are. The debt that's known, that is openly displayed on the balance sheets, comes to about $2 trillion, which isn't peanuts but that might be manageable. But the biggest problem is with the debt that's unknown but that still must be serviced. In other words, it's the debt arising from the murky shadow banking arena.

Shadow Banking

Shadow banking operates outside the regulated banking system. It provides loans, at high interest rates, to borrowers who don't qualify for loans from within the regular banking system.

In late 2018, Moody's estimated that shadow banking in China approached $9 trillion (which was down from $10 trillion earlier in the year). The LGFVs accounted for a hefty portion. In fact, hidden debt held by LGFVs is thought to be more than twice the debt shown on their balance sheets. This suggests that overall LGFV debt could be as much as 60 percent of China's GDP. It's a big number, and the bulk of it is essentially invisible.

The main source of the off-balance-sheet debt held by LGFVs is lending from regional banks that resorted to questionable ways of raising additional funding. In particular, the banks have offered off-balance-sheet investments known as *wealth management products* (WMPs). Their attraction is their high returns, far higher than what a bank's customers would get on their deposits. But they're riskier, because they are not guaranteed by the government, although some WMP investors apparently have believed that they were.

In essence, banks raise money to lend to LGFVs by offering high interest rates to bank customers on WMPs that don't show up on the banks' balance sheets; the banks then turn around and lend the money to the LGFVs at high interest rates. It creates potential risks throughout the system—for the LGFVs, the banks, and customers alike.

Shadow banking is widely considered a major problem for China. One thing to realize, though, is that not all shadow debt is bad debt or associated with dicey products such as WMPs. Some is funded by credible sources such as wealthy individuals (trust loans) and solidly rated corporations (a portion of entrusted loans). Moreover, funding from these sources is being capped at current levels and so will decline over time. The riskier sources, such as person-to-person lending, are being effectively terminated by the government.

Also, LGFVs don't account for all of Chinese shadow lending. Some shadow debt is held by private companies that are relatively unleveraged and have strong growth prospects. They nonetheless had to resort to shadow banking because even well-situated private companies can find it hard to borrow from large banks, which favor SOEs.

China has been working, with some success, to reduce its shadow banking problem, and Bloomberg has reported a decline in the percentage of loans that originate from shadow banking. One step was to order banks that offer WMPs to tell investors that contrary to what many assumed, the products are not government guaranteed. As a result, WMPs have begun to decline. Other sources of funding, such as structured deposits, which tie higher interest rates to macro variables such as the price of gold or the exchange rate of the yuan, have been gaining favor. These funding sources appear on bank balance sheets, have contingent rather than promised returns, and are implicitly backed by the central government.

China isn't the only country with a shadow banking sector. In April 2019, a CNBC.com piece estimated that worldwide shadow banking amounts to about $51 trillion. At most, China, assuming no reductions from the 2018 figure of $9 trillion, would account for about 17.5 percent of that. And given that shadow loans in China have either stopped growing or been cut sharply, its share could be below 17.5 percent. The Financial Stability Board's estimate is that China represents about 16 percent of the world's total.

The country with the largest share of shadow banking? It's the United States, whose share tops 30 percent. Remember, it was the United States and its shadow banking that almost cratered the entire financial system in 2008–2009. Prior to then, the United States had made no efforts to curb shadow banking.

Other Considerations

One reason to think that China's debt is less of a Damocles' sword than often portrayed is that most of it is internal. Debt held by foreigners amounts to only 15 percent of China's GDP, one of the lowest percentages in the world, among developed and developing countries alike. This is consistent with the high value China places on self-reliance, and it means that foreigners can't dictate monetary policies.

The only other nation where foreign-held debt is below 100 percent of GDP is Japan, at 70 percent. Japan's yen is often considered a haven currency just because of the relatively small portion of Japanese debt held by foreigners, yet as a percentage of GDP, Japan's foreign-owned debt is four and a half times China's level. For the United States, foreign-owned debt is 115 percent of GDP and rising.

Another relevant figure is that China's household debt, while rising in recent years, stands at more than 55 percent of GDP. This is a level that most other countries would love to have. The largest portion of it is mortgages, and on average, mortgages in China are based on much higher equity than in other countries. Also attesting to the relative financial stability of Chinese households, China's household savings rate is 36 percent of household income, far and away the highest among major economies.

A final thought is that you could reasonably view SOEs and LGFVs as government rather than corporate debt, which changes the calculus. Many of these companies have the potential to generate huge amounts of money. If you add SOE debt to other government debt, government debt jumps to more than 120 percent of GDP and, if you are pessimistic especially about local SOEs, perhaps as high as 150 percent of GDP.

But whether government debt is 120 or 150 percent of GDP, the point is that much of it relates to enterprises that are vital for the country's infrastructure and future growth. The debt not only is guaranteed by the government, but it's also backed by the tremendous asset base many of the SOEs have.

In other words, it's debt that will help fund future growth. In the United States, the lion's share of government debt represents IOUs owed to the public to pay for entitlement programs. There is no way to grow out of this debt. In fact, faulty assumptions about life expectancies and poor management of healthcare virtually ensure that it will grow as the money contributed by workers becomes increasingly insufficient. Inevitably, coping with this shortfall will mean more taxes and eventually borrowing more from abroad, debt the world will have to trust we eventually will pay back.

15
The Start of America's Decline

IN HIS BRILLIANT and elegiac song, "American Tune," released in 1973, Paul Simon lamented: "we've lived so well so long, still, when I think of the road we're traveling on, I wonder what's gone wrong." Clearly, the song was informed by the turmoil of that era, including the Vietnam War, political assassinations, and Watergate. Probably the last thing on Simon's mind was President Nixon's 1971 decision to delink the dollar from gold. But if not the stuff to inspire song lyrics, that decision was in many ways every bit as fateful as the more violent events racking the United States.

A lot of data support the idea that 1971 marks a dividing line between America's good times and the start of a long decline persisting into the present. The snapping of the gold/dollar link wasn't the only factor, but it was more complicit in that decline than is generally realized.

It helped foster an array of ills, including an unhealthy focus on short-term gratification, rising income inequalities, anemic productivity gains, the expansion of heavy unsecured consumer debt, our contorted healthcare system, and deteriorating public education. It bears a lot of blame for burgeoning bureaucracies and an explosion in regulations that went along with the rise of a large financial/legal class that commandeers most of the country's wealth while contributing little to productivity.

Others also have pointed to 1971 as marking an important before-and-after dividing line but have cited different reasons. Hedrick Smith in his book, *Who Stole the American Dream?* (Random House, 2012), picks the year as a decisive turning point. But he focuses on the famous—or infamous—memo written in 1971 by Lewis Powell, Jr., when he was still a corporate lawyer, before Nixon named him to the Supreme Court. Powell urged businesses to mobilize aggressively against unions and consumer crusaders so as to maximize profits, executive salaries, and shareholder returns.

Powell's memorandum no doubt influenced corporate thinking and actions. But I think that delinking the dollar from gold had even broader repercussions, ones we continue to feel today.

Whatever the most important proximate cause, beginning in the 1970s, the United States took a wrong turn. By one measure after another, over the past half century, we have slipped. This has left us ill-positioned—however much chest thumping the United States still might engage in—to effectively counter China's push to establish itself as the hegemon in the East, including its plans to elevate gold.

The irony is hard to miss. If I'm right that it's more than coincidental that America began changing for the worse once the gold/dollar link was snapped, then, in some variant of karma, a thread leads from that decision to the big bull market in gold that lies ahead.

Snapping the Link

The Bretton Woods Conference that thrashed out the post–World War II international monetary order sought to establish an orderly system, one that by fostering global trade would ensure peaceful relations among nations. Its achievements included creating the International Monetary Fund (IMF) and the precursor to the World Bank. And it set forth rules for how currencies would interact in the conduct of international trade. A centerpiece was anointing the U.S. dollar as the world's reserve currency, pegging it to gold at the rate of $35 per ounce of gold.

All other major currencies were pegged to the dollar and allowed to trade only within very narrow limits. Ditto for gold, which could trade on foreign exchanges but was restricted to a narrow band. While Bretton Woods mandated that any country could redeem its dollars for gold, initially other countries had little reason to do so. U.S. gold reserves—about 20,000 metric tons in 1950, or around 70 percent of total global gold reserves—were roughly double the world's dollar holdings, so there was no reason to question the dollar's soundness. And with international trade transactions denominated in dollars, countries needed to make sure that they had sufficient dollar reserves.

Little more than two decades later, U.S. gold reserves had declined by over 50 percent, to around $11 billion. Meanwhile, the dollar holdings of trading partners had grown. Germany, France, and Italy, for example, had around $25 billion in dollars. If they chose to exchange even a small fraction of those holdings for gold, they could sweep up all the gold the United States held.

In other words, by the start of the 1970s, the United States no longer had enough gold to make good its pledge to exchange dollars for gold on request. This essentially forced Nixon to delink the dollar from gold, which he did in August 1971.

But the dollar continued to be the global reserve currency and to enjoy the many privileges that conferred, including, crucially, having commodities priced in dollars. On the surface, it appeared that little had changed. This appearance was deceptive.

Exorbitant Privilege

One change was that the United States was freed of any restraints on its fiscal and monetary activities. As long as the dollar was yoked to gold, the United States had to apply a steady hand to monetary policy in order to exchange dollars for gold at a constant rate. With gold out of the picture, that restraint vanished.

We became like teenagers in possession of a parent's credit card, going on spending sprees without worrying about footing the bill. We printed dollars for anything and everything, from fighting wars to spending on social programs, without needing to make difficult choices or consider longer-term consequences. The assumption was that if problems arose, we could always spend more money to fix them. U.S. money supply growth soared after 1971.

But other countries continued to want our dollars and buy our bonds because they needed dollars to conduct international trade. Particularly significant was our deal with the Saudis to price oil in dollars. Guaranteed demand for the dollar meant that we didn't have to pay high real interest rates or worry that our high debt would translate into the kind of hyperinflation that wracked nations like Argentina.

No other country had such "exorbitant privilege." If any other country tried to print its way out of slow growth, it would have set off a vicious circle in which ever-higher inflation led to ever-great drops in the value of the currency. As the country with the reserve currency, however, the United States had a free pass. It could now print as much money as it needed, whether to overcome recessionary forces such as the OPEC oil embargo in 1973 or simply to fund any initiative that Congress and the president wanted to pass.

All good? Not really. If the United States seemed to be having its cake and eating it too, freedom from fiscal and monetary restraint came at a cost. Over the years, it has proved to be profoundly corrosive. Most basically, it has led to the triumph of short-term gratification over long-term planning, a distortion that has rippled throughout the economy and society and left us increasingly vulnerable even as seemingly we have remained king of the mountain.

A Golden Age . . .

By all key economic indicators, the decades between the end of World War II and the 1970s were a golden age for the United States. Between 1949 and 1973, productivity in the United States grew at an average annualized rate of 2.6 percent, which roughly matched growth in real compensation. Thanks to the magic of compounding, in those years, both productivity and real incomes advanced by 90 percent.

It was a time of optimism and forward thinking, of can-do spirit. In those years, America could commit to grand long-term projects with multiple benefits for the country as a whole. The interstate highway system, which resulted from the Federal Aid Highway Act of 1956, is one enduring example. The legislation authorized construction of 41,000 miles of highways spanning the nation, allocating $26 billion—more than half a trillion dollars in today's dollars—to pay for it. Besides knitting together the country and fostering a more efficient flow of vehicles, it was meant to ensure that Americans could evacuate their cities if they came under atomic attack. Thus it was deemed essential for national security.

It was a massive infrastructure project that arguably did more to improve the economy's productivity than any other effort. It has been estimated that every dollar spent on the interstate highway system generated at least six dollars in increased productivity. It's hard to imagine the United States without it—we would be simply a collection of poorly connected cities.

That era also saw the seemingly endless scientific accomplishments of Bell Labs, which was part of AT&T. AT&T was a very different company back then. It was a monopoly that worked in close partnership with the government, essentially controlling communications, mostly telephony, throughout the United States. It was both a vertical and horizontal monopoly, with its Western Electric subsidiary manufacturing much of the nation's communications gear.

Operating under the aegis of Western Electric, Bell Labs functioned as an independent research organization. Its projects ranged from the most practical to the most theoretical, and it was under no pressure to complete projects within a fixed time limit. Budgets were flexible, and projects were rarely, if ever, terminated because they became too expensive. Many Bell Labs scientists also worked in academia or government, especially the Defense Department.

Bell Labs was a quintessential example of what pure research is all about. The number and breadth of the successful projects it rolled out give it a claim to being the greatest incubator of research ever. It was responsible for the transistor, the laser, the internet (developed jointly with the Defense Department's DARPA), superconductivity, and much more.

Bell scientists won many Nobel Prizes, including one for the first substantiation of the Big Bang theory of the universe. Software developed by Bell scientists is the progenitor of much of today's software. Information theory, which is still the theoretical backbone of virtually all our current information technologies, resulted from the research of Bell scientist Claude Shannon, which he published as a master's thesis for MIT.

Our space program incorporated a lot of Bell Labs' technology. Bell Labs was one reason we were able to so quickly catch up to and then surpass the Russians in the space race after the shock of Russia's launch of *Sputnik*. The moon landing was the most dramatic manifestation of our willingness to go all out on ambitious long-term projects.

The government's Bell Labs role went beyond its generous financial backing for AT&T and its direct collaboration on many projects. The original transistor was developed for radar in World War II and used in communication devices such as radios and televisions. Through additional research, it evolved into a replacement for the very bulky vacuum tubes in computers. If you're as old as I am, you may have nostalgic memories of radios with transistors so large that they were visible in the back of the radio.

Today, some 50 billion transistors fit into the space originally occupied by just one. Probably the most important factor in this shrinkage was the government's willingness to order massive numbers of transistors, allowing manufacturers to rapidly advance along a learning curve.

. . . And Its End

In the years after 1971, important measures of economic health began to slide. Standard measures of productivity growth continued to advance, although at a slightly slower pace. But wages for workers began diverging from productivity growth in a historic way, leading to growing inequalities that would become ever-more evident in coming decades.

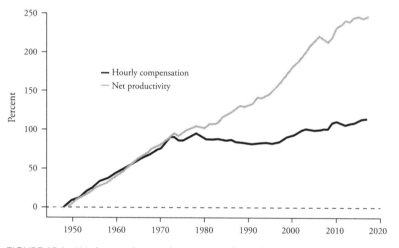

FIGURE 15.1   Worker pay has not kept pace with productivity since the 1970s.
Source: Economic Policy Institute.

According to the Bureau of Labor Statistics, average real compensation grew by less than 1 percent a year for nonfarm workers (over 99 percent of the economy), while productivity climbed by about 2.2 percent. In other words, real wages on a yearly basis trailed the economic value of goods created by more than 50 percent. You can trace a clear path from the loss of monetary discipline after 1971 to that drastic shrinkage in workers' participation in the economy's growth.

As the economic indicators began pointing to an economy starting to fail more people, the glory days of scientific research and grand projects were ebbing as well. In 1982, the AT&T monopoly was broken up, with the idea of promoting competition in the long-distance phone business. AT&T lost its competitive advantage, and Western Electric, focused on pleasing investors, turned away from pursuing long-term open-ended projects. In the mid-1990s, it became part of Lucent, which in the early twenty-first century, in the aftermath of the bursting of the dot.com bubble, became part of a European telecom. Today, Bell Labs, though still doing good research, is a shadow of its former self and in any case no longer belongs to the United States.

As for grand infrastructure projects, it's fair to say that we never again attempted anything remotely comparable to the interstate highway system. In fact, as discussed in Chapter 4, we're not even maintaining the infrastructure we have, including our highways. Today the overwhelming bulk of new infrastructure created in the United States originates within the private sector and isn't geared toward improving overall public welfare.

If 1971 marked a distinct dividing line, though, it didn't come out of the blue. After all, Nixon had to end the Bretton Woods arrangement because of the sharp decline in U.S. gold reserves that already had taken place, which forced his hand.

That decline had started as early as 1960 when John F. Kennedy was elected president promising lower interest rates and more government spending on social programs. Investors started to anticipate that more dollar printing in the context of a supply of gold that would not keep pace would lead to the dollar becoming overvalued.

Gold, which traded in London, began to rise, briefly topping $40 an ounce. This incentivized governments to exchange their dollars for gold at $35 an ounce and sell it in London for a profit, and U.S. gold reserves declined.

The British government and eventually other Western countries were tasked with managing the situation by selling their own gold reserves when prices moved above $35.20 an ounce and buying when gold traded below $35.08 an ounce. The upper end of the $35.08 to $35.20 range was too low to attract arbitrageurs because of the costs associated with exchanging dollars for gold and selling the gold.

In the middle to late 1960s, the situation worsened sharply as spending rose on both the growing war effort in Vietnam and President Johnson's Great Society programs. Inflationary pressures began to build. There was no escaping that the dollar, fixed at $35 to an ounce to gold, was overvalued. As dollar printing accelerated, so did outflows of gold.

With the election of Richard Nixon, the United States effectively gave up any efforts at restoring the kind of discipline that could have protected the gold standard. In early 1970, Nixon appointed Arthur Burns as head of the Federal Reserve. Though the Fed was supposedly an independent body, Nixon relentlessly pressured Burns to do nothing that could cause unemployment to spike.

Lower unemployment fosters rising inflation and thus a weaker dollar because when prices rise, a dollar buys less. Nixon's line in the sand was 4 percent unemployment. Any time unemployment threatened to move higher, he expected the Fed to print more money so as to promote growth—and inflation be damned. To put it another way, Nixon ordered the Fed to abandon economic discipline. The Fed obliged, and our gold reserves began to drop at a rapid pace, culminating, in 1971, with the dollar and gold being formally delinked.

The lack of economic discipline that accelerated from 1971 on infected many spheres of American life. It permitted distortions that over time have insidiously gnawed away at the underpinnings of American society, sapping some of our vitality and focus. One repercussion is that we've been left ill-positioned to rise to this century's challenge of an emergent China.

Healthcare in the United States

I'd bet a lot of money that politicians in other countries don't go around promising to make their countries' healthcare system just like ours, that is, to create an expensive hodgepodge of private insurers and bureaucratic middlemen, to force millions of people to pay high out-of-pocket costs along with high premiums, to offer a plethora of confusing insurance policies that even more confusingly get rewritten every year, and to bill patients thousands of dollars for a surgical procedure performed by a doctor in a patient's network simply because an out-of-network doctor dropped by for an unasked-for five-minute consultation. (Yes, I'm speaking from personal experience.) A system that still leaves millions of Americans with no insurance at all.

No, it doesn't add up to an appealing political platform.

The United States has some outstanding world-class hospitals and many brilliant, dedicated, and caring doctors. But no one could argue with a straight face that the overall system makes a whole lot of sense.

Hard data support this assessment. Per-capita healthcare spending in the United States now tops $10,000, the highest of any country in the world. It's more than 25 percent higher than number two, Luxembourg, and more than twice that of many developed countries.

As a percentage of gross domestic product (GDP), the United States again is an outlier, with healthcare accounting for nearly 20 percent of GDP. No other country even makes the teens.

While we spend more, our health outcomes are worse. The most basic measure of a country's healthcare system is life expectancies. According to the 2017 World Population Survey, the United States ranks forty-sixth in the world, with life expectancies here averaging a bit under 80 years. This is worse than both Cuba and Lebanon.

In sum, when it comes to healthcare, arguably never in modern history has so much money been spent on human well-being with so little in return.

It wasn't always like this. In 1960, Americans aged 65 and older—men and women alike—had longer life expectancies than senior citizens in six other major developed countries. This continued to be true in 1970. Today, retirement-age Americans, both men and women, have fewer years ahead of them than new retirees in those other six countries.

Have you ever wondered how we ended up with the healthcare system we have? It has its origins in the early 1970s, when there was a battle royal between Senator Ted Kennedy, chair of the Senate's Health Care Committee, and President Nixon. Kennedy was a fierce advocate for a relatively straightforward universal single-payer system, the kind adopted in some form or another by virtually all developed countries. Single-payer systems offer the advantage of being fair and transparent. Costs can easily be assessed and, if necessary, controlled.

Nixon countered with a proposal for a far more complicated system. It offered enhanced publicly funded coverage for low-wage workers side by side with a complex system of mandates and incentives for employers to offer coverage. There were some attempts to work out a compromise, but politics and a lack of a sense of urgency about ultimate costs led to a system that on any rational grounds should have been a nonstarter.

The emergence of healthcare insurance companies was as close as the United States came to pooling healthcare costs as a negotiating tactic with providers. But the insurance companies added a massive layer of costs. As publicly traded companies, their mandates were profits. Executives who could produce those profits and push the stock price up reaped huge salaries and bonuses. Eventually, other layers of profit-seeking companies entered the mix, such as pharmacy benefit managers and drug distributors.

The lack of fiscal discipline was instrumental in permitting such an unwieldy and inefficient system to come into existence. Policymakers were under no pressure to think in terms of lean and mean. It's a frustrating illustration of how the freedom to spend was anything but productive.

And, of course, the malignant effects persist today, with healthcare a perennial worry for Americans, an expense for businesses, and a divisive political flashpoint. The fierce pushback over the decades to all efforts to revamp healthcare in the United States is telling. It shows how once a system gets entrenched, it's incredibly hard to dislodge, with politics and special interests posing daunting hurdles. President

Obama's Affordable Care Act made a dent in some of the worst features of the system, but think how difficult it was to accomplish even that. Getting it right back in the early 1970s would have made an inestimable contribution to American life. Less freedom to print dollars would have made that a lot more likely to have occurred.

Trailing in Education

A country's education system may matter even more than healthcare to economic vibrancy and an ability to compete. Here, too, the United States spends more and achieves less.

According to the Census Bureau and the Organisation for Economic Co-operation and Development (OECD), the United States spends about $25,000 per year per student below college level. Only Luxembourg, with a population of fewer than 700,000 people and among the richest countries in the world in per-capita income, spends more. Combined U.S. federal and state annual spending on education amounts to more than $100 billion.

But teacher pay in the United States is only in the middle of the pack for all countries. The high per-student spending isn't going toward offering salaries high enough to attract and keep the most qualified teachers. Rather, it supports a vast educational bureaucracy that is removed from the real goal of education, which should be to give students a foundation of knowledge and skills and an ability to think and learn. Many teachers would surely argue, in fact, that educational bureaucracies only make their own jobs harder to perform well.

Unlike healthcare spending, which on a per-capita basis and as a percentage of GDP accelerated sharply in the 1970s and beyond, spending on education in the United States didn't show the same inflection point. But there are signs that the United States began to shortchange actual educational outcomes while indulging a spending-for-the-sake-of-spending mentality.

Economist Jonathan Rothwell focused on the mismatch between spending and results in a December 2016 report for the Brookings

Institution titled, "The Declining Productivity of Education." He wrote: "Like any other sphere of economic activity, the productivity of the education sector depends on the relationship between how much it generates in value—learning, in this case—relative to its costs. Unfortunately, productivity is way down."

Between 1980 and 2015, according to Rothwell, spending on education in the United States rose at about a 6 percent annualized rate—roughly double the rate of inflation. The rise in spending was across the board, applying to public and private schools alike and to pre-K through secondary school (usually high school). Spending on college rose more than 11-fold over the same period, an annualized rate of more than 7 percent.

But Americans weren't becoming better educated. Rothwell's data show that the last generation of Americans with literacy and math scores above the average for OECD countries came of age in the early 1970s. By the decade's end, our numeracy scores sharply lagged, and our literary scores were about average. Although skills in both areas have been rising each generation, gains in the United States have been smaller than for any other OECD country.

Other evidence further supports the view that educational outcomes in the United States have lagged. Every three years, the Program for International Student Assessment (PISA) conducts a worldwide assessment of the scholastic performance of students across 70 nations, including the developed world and much of the developing world. It tests for math, science, and reading skills. In 2018, China was first, Singapore second, Macau third, Hong Kong fourth, and Japan sixth. The United States was in twenty-fifth place.

The growing numbers of administrators means that teachers are getting a shrinking portion of the education spending pie. Most teachers, even at the primary school level, need advanced degrees, an expensive process. The low pay helps explain why teaching doesn't attract the most talented graduates and why higher overall per-student spending on education still leaves students here performing even below students in a growing part of the developing world.

Inadequate education at elementary through high school levels leaves too many Americans ill-equipped to obtain the higher education essential to compete in today's world. This is tragic not just for them. It's a drag on the U.S. economy as a whole and on our standing in the world, another edge for China in gaining ascendancy on many fronts where we used to dominate.

Lagging Wages, Rising Bureaucracy

Lack of fiscal discipline has shown up in the overall economy, not just in specific sectors such as health and education. A basic measure of an economy's health is labor productivity, worker output per hour. Rising productivity lets workers earn more without causing inflation, because the additional wages are matched by increased output. This foundational measure more than doubled between 1947 and 1973, an annualized growth rate of nearly 3 percent. Wages doubled as well.

As noted earlier, starting in the early 1970s, while productivity continued to advance, though at a slightly lower rate, wages stopped keeping up. Since then, despite continued gains in productivity, measures of real median income have barely budged. In other words, for nearly half a century, U.S. workers haven't gotten the benefits of their labor.

Figure 15.1 on page 159 shows this dramatic divergence. It covers the entire economy, including both services and manufacturing, but let's talk about productivity in terms of manufacturing, which is simpler to measure. With manufacturing, the whole idea is simply to produce more of a concrete item. Measuring productivity in the service sector is murkier, with no hard and fast criteria.

But it turns out that the manufacturing sector in and of itself, in terms of measured productivity, is representative of the economy as a whole. Productivity has advanced by a little more than 2.5 percent a year since the early 1970s, while real wage gains have gained just a bit more than 1 percent a year.

The question is why. One answer is that as wages began to trail productivity in the early 1970s, nonlabor unit costs were starting to accelerate. Nonlabor costs are just what the name implies. They are any cost related to producing a product other than labor (and excluding profits). They include salaries of administrators, legal expenses incurred to ensure compliance with environmental and safety standards, and so on.

A significant portion of the higher nonlabor costs came from the growing burden of complying with a steadily growing slew of government regulations. The freedom to spend with more abandon that began in the early 1970s gave government more room to expand its oversight. It did so by issuing slews of new guidelines regulating businesses, adding layers of complexity. Bureaucracies burgeoned at both the government and corporate levels to enforce the rules and ensure compliance. The trend had started with President Johnson's Great Society but accelerated in the 1970s.

Decrying bureaucracy and excessive government regulation often is viewed as the purview of conservatives. Liberals typically are seen as more apt to expand regulations intended to protect consumers and the environment. This may be a fair characterization of the politics of regulation, but it obscures some of the complexities of the onset of the regulatory age.

By adding to corporations' nonlabor costs, burgeoning regulations took away from spending on labor itself. All the money devoted to lawyers and accountants and other white-collar higher-paid employees sopped up the productivity gains that in earlier times went to lower-level workers.

Ronald Bird, a senior regulatory analyst with the U.S. Chamber of Commerce, pinpointed some of the issues in a 2015 article. According to Bird, federal regulations grew from 9,745 pages in 1950 to more than 174,496 pages through 2014. The result, he said, has made regulatory compliance "a major cost center for companies. Allocating scarce resources to regulatory compliance inevitably competes with labor and capital available for production, innovation, and investment, thus impairing economic performance."

If regulation has drastically accelerated since the early 1970s, deregulation has too. The two are often seen as polar opposites. After all, regulation gives the government more control over businesses. Deregulation reduces or removes government control over a particular industry, with the goal of encouraging competition and benefiting consumers. Airlines, natural gas, trucking, and, most important, telephony have all been deregulated in recent decades.

But if excessive regulation has had unintended consequences of hurting the workers and consumers they were intended to protect, acting as a drag on wage growth, deregulation at times has hurt the same groups. Whereas competition can lead to lower prices and better products, it also can leave employees in a newly deregulated industry much more vulnerable. And for consumers, it can lead to shortcuts such as less testing of new products. These sorts of factors are accentuated by a society ever more focused on short-term gains, a focus that is especially evident in the ballooning financial/legal sector, which I look at in Chapter 16.

16

The Unproductive
Financial Sector

MY FIRST FORAY into investing came in the 1960s when I was in college. I had bought shares in a technology company called Informatics. To track its progress, I'd check the financial pages each morning. I wasn't aiming for a quick profit. My thought was to hold onto the shares at least until I graduated. I also had some idea that by supporting an innovative company with a lot of potential, I was contributing in some small way to the good of the country. We were in the midst of the postwar bull market that had begun in mid-1949, and I ended up doing pretty well.

Back then, many Americans participated in the market with the same notion of doing good—supporting the economy—while doing well. Of course, some of the companies being supported may have been doing less than stellar things, from polluting the environment to selling tobacco. But at least the system had a rationale that made sense. It served a valuable economic purpose, giving companies access to public financing while enhancing investor wealth. It created value, with widespread benefits to the companies and their workers and to individual investors around the country. The system wasn't rigged against the little person.

That post–World War II bull market started with the Dow Jones Industrial Average near 160 and ended in early 1966 with the Dow some five points short of 1,000. Few at the time imagined it would take 16 years before the Dow would succeed in decisively breaking through the psychologically important 1,000 barrier.

August 13, 1982, marked the start of the second postwar bull market, an even more historic rise than the first, and one that continues through the present day. Corrections notwithstanding, including some that were deep, the Dow has risen 30-fold since 1982.

This second postwar bull market, though, has a less benign aspect to it than the first. Its backdrop has been an America increasingly enamored of short-term gains and abandoning fiscal discipline while embracing a wildly excessive regulatory regime. The second bull market in many ways encapsulates—and I think bears a hefty share of the blame for—a lot that has continued to go wrong.

Once again, there's plenty of irony to point to. On the surface, the long-running bull market in stocks that began in 1982 seems a sign of American capitalism's glory. But it also can be seen as part of an erosion of our economic foundations that has left us less resilient and less able to counter China—and therefore a factor in the coming bull market in gold.

Inflation, Stocks, and Volcker

One thing the two postwar bull markets have in common is that both unfolded during eras of low inflation. This is not a coincidence. Low inflation is the stock market's friend. Investors like the clarity that it offers. They like to be able to look to the future and see that companies can grow. For investors, inflation is a cloud that blocks their view of the future. The higher inflation goes, the denser is the cloud. By contrast, low and declining inflation goes hand in hand with a longer-term horizon for valuing assets.

This is why, during times of low inflation, price/earnings (P/E) ratios of stocks rise, boosting share prices. Public companies report profits every quarter. Those profits, the ones already booked, matter to investors. But investors care even more about whether a company can continue to generate profits and do so at a rising rate. When inflation is low, investors have more confidence that companies will be able to deliver. In other words, when inflation is low, investors place a higher value on future earnings, raising P/E ratios.

Of course, inflation isn't the only factor in a stock's P/E ratio. Company- and industry-specific factors also play a role. For instance, if investors anticipate that the government will issue stricter regulations affecting the healthcare industry, P/E ratios for healthcare companies would likely drop, pushing their share prices down.

When it comes to the broader big-picture outlook, however, nothing—not even bond yields—correlates more strongly with P/E ratios than inflation. More generally, inflation is the foundational metric that determines how nearly all financial assets are valued, including stocks and bonds.

The lower inflation is, the surer you can be that growth reflects rising productivity and/or rising unit growth, factors that can be analyzed in terms of their sustainability. Low inflation also makes it easier for companies to plan for the future because they have a better idea of future costs and profit margins. Low inflation also means policymakers have room to stimulate the economy if growth should falter.

During the first postwar bull market, between 1949 and 1966, the Consumer Price Index (CPI) climbed at an annualized rate of a touch below 2 percent. Inflation also has been consistently low in the second bull market: Between 1982 and 2018, the CPI rose at an annualized rate of 2.6 percent. The Standard and Poor's 500 Index (S&P 500) average P/E ratio today is around 20, some two and a half times higher than its 1982 level.

But in between the two bull markets, inflation looked very different. Between 1966 and 1970, as the federal government began spending on Vietnam and social programs, inflation rose at an annualized rate of 4.8 percent. And once the gold standard was abandoned, inflation went on a historic tear. It rose at an average annualized rate of 7.8 percent and at times hit double digits, such as when OPEC pushed oil prices from below $5 a barrel in the early 1970s to as high as $40 in the early 1980s.

As inflation surged, unemployment reached a high of 9 percent in 1975. The recession of 1973–1975 became known as *stagflation*—a sorry combination of high inflation and high unemployment. Though the economy began to grow again, inflation higher and during long stretches much higher than 5 percent became the norm.

Not surprisingly, during those years, stocks struggled, and P/E ratios dropped. By mid-1982, the value of stocks adjusted for inflation was little changed from the mid-1966 level (and down about 30 percent from the mid-1964 level). In the 12 months prior to July 1982, with inflation averaging almost 9 percent, the P/E ratio of the S&P 500 averaged lower than 8.

Ultimately, though, inflation met its match in the formidable personage of Paul Volcker. Appointed head of the Federal Reserve by President Carter in 1979 and reappointed by President Reagan four years later, Volcker will forever be known as the slayer of the inflation of the 1970s and early 1980s. But he had to battle mightily to earn those spurs.

When Volcker became Fed chairman in 1979, inflation had reached 11 percent and was threatening to move ever higher in a vicious circle, with consumers buying all they could in the present to avoid paying higher prices later. Under such a dynamic, the more that consumers spend, the greater the upward pressure on prices, leading to more inflation and more incentive to spend in the moment, and on and on. In Volcker's first 11 months as Fed chairman, inflation's momentum, buttressed by higher oil prices because of the Iran-Iraq war, pushed inflation to a peacetime high of above 14 percent.

With single-minded focus and the steely willingness to implement a draconian monetary policy that sent interest rates soaring, Volcker brought the process to a halt. From its peak of 14.8 percent in March

1980, inflation fell to below 3 percent by 1983. Under Volcker, the Fed raised the federal funds rate to a peak of 20 percent in June 1981; the prime rate rose to 21.5 percent. The collateral damage was the vicious 1980–1982 recession, during which the unemployment rate rose above 10 percent.

The low inflation that Volcker engineered, combined with strong prospects for growth, revitalized the moribund stock market. Stocks have been in a bull market, punctuated by corrections, ever since because low inflation has become an ingrained economic mantra. In the years between 1982 and 2018, as the Dow rose 30-fold, the CPI rose at an annualized rate of 2.6 percent.

Chapter 18 looks more closely at inflation, which is far more complex than just the CPI. In fact, in recent decades, the CPI has camouflaged price rises that disproportionately affect lower-income Americans, with the effect of widening and reinforcing income inequality.

Here, though, it's enough to note that the postwar bull markets in stocks have gone hand in hand with low inflation, as measured by the CPI. From the perspective of corporate earnings and share prices, this was more than good enough to provide the oxygen for heady gains.

Why do I see the second postwar bull market as far less benign than the earlier one? Among other things, it epitomizes the country's short-term outlook and its focus on instant gratification. It has elevated the financial sector in ways that are anything but beneficial. It has worsened income inequality and siphoned off valuable resources, including human brainpower, that could have been put to better use.

It's worth homing in on how the burgeoning financial sector has been integral to America's decline.

A Really Bad Roommate

To convey some of the distortions that have emerged, I'll start with a simple analogy. Imagine that you're a college student and that you share an apartment with two roommates. You all contribute to the rent, the food, the utilities, etc. on an equal basis. Moreover, each of you has particular skills that you apply to maintain the apartment in sparkling condition and to live healthy lives. One of you likes to cook, one of you is a whiz at cleaning, and one of you is meticulous about doing laundry and ironing. (Yes, obviously, this is a total fantasy.)

Now imagine that the roommate who does the cooking gets hold of some new appliances that he says will result in better meals at lower cost. Because of these putative improvements, he argues that his own contribution to apartment life should be more highly valued. He proposes that he should be rewarded by getting to eat half the food instead of one-third, including all the desserts; that he should have exclusive use of the living room; and that his share of the rent should go down.

You and the other roommate, a bit befuddled, go along. It takes the two of you a while to realize that not only are you getting less food and paying more, but its quality is actually no better than before. In fact, it might even be worse. It's true that the vaunted appliances can chop food faster, but they don't make it taste any better, and some of the time they turn it into mush. Somehow you and the other noncook roommate have found yourselves in a position where you're eating less while shelling out more money and being confined to your bedrooms. Meanwhile, the third roommate has been getting rich (as well as fat).

Pretty ugly, right? It's not all that out of line with how in recent decades the financial sector as a whole and many of those who work within it have accumulated outsized wealth while doing nothing genuinely useful or productive to justify it. Rather than make an actual contribution to the economy, the financial sector has dazzled and befuddled with shiny complex objects that benefit only the financial sector itself, not most investors or the country as a whole.

If this sounds harsh, let's look at some of the data. They start with the fact that compared with earlier times, the financial sector now constitutes a much bigger part of the overall economy. As of 2017, according to the U.S. Bureau of Economic Analysis, the financial sector generated nearly 28 percent of the overall economy's profits compared with less than 14 percent in 1981. Compensation in the financial sector has risen sevenfold to above $1 trillion a year and represents more than 10 percent of total economy-wide compensation, as wages in the financial sector have risen compared with wages in the rest of the economy.

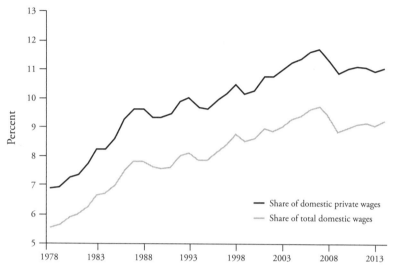

FIGURE 16.1 Growing wage share of finance, insurance, and real estate.
Source: Center for Economic and Policy Research (CEPR).

What's wrong with this? It's that the rising flood of money that has been sucked up by the financial sector and caused it to swell as a proportion of the overall economy largely reflects nonproductive developments that benefit only those within the sector itself. As compensation for those within the sector soars and profits generated by the sector rise, people on the outside increasingly have struggled, leading to widening inequalities and all the ills they bring.

In part, the sector has ballooned because of the explosive growth in regulations I discussed in Chapter 15. Complying with them requires the services of endless numbers of lawyers, accountants, and managers, who get paid well for doing things that are essentially self-referential and create nothing of value, nothing that promotes actual growth. All these groups benefit from the rising complexity that characterizes U.S. life, getting big sums to manage it. But the rest of the country suffers as the complexity gums up the works and makes real progress elusive while vastly widening inequality.

Excessive regulations aren't the whole story, however. The financial sector began to swell in the 1980s after inflation was tamed. Prior to that, all the dollars that were being printed once the dollar/gold link was broken had gone into chasing goods as prices kept rising. But once Volcker broke the back of inflation, those dollars began chasing financial assets instead. Stocks went up. And looking for more ways to profit, financial institutions rushed to create all sorts of complex and often risky new financial instruments that would generate fees and amplify their returns.

Not So Kindly After All

Meanwhile, the growing size and complexity of the financial sector have benefited neither the country as a whole nor the typical investor. Wealth management and investment advisory firms, for instance, make up one segment of the financial sector. They run great ads on TV that make you think that if only you engaged one of those wise, kindly advisers who seem to take such a remarkably personal interest in their clients' needs, you, too, could live your life to the fullest before sailing off into the sunset. The firms rake in big fees for convincing investors about this idea. Yet a 2017 study by Standard & Poor's concluded that only around 5 percent of wealth advisors outperform stock index funds.

An index fund, of course, simply mirrors all the stocks in that particular index. It's the very definition of passive investing. You don't need an adviser to help you with it. Thus, all the countless numbers of investors who are willing to pay fees to advisers to pick stocks for them are betting that the advisers will produce better results than if the investors had simply put their money into an index fund mirroring the S&P 500. Nineteen of 20 of those investors will lose that bet. They will pay extra to do worse. And yet the average compensation of those in the advisory business is $275,000 a year.

Reporter Brian Tanguay described these distortions in the following apt words: "between investors and the market sits a layer of middlemen who earn fees, commissions, and rebates from order flow and volume. This labyrinth adds little actual value to the market or the larger economy; middlemen profit from the complexity they have nurtured and sustained—and defend with every resource at their disposal."

And devastatingly, at enormous cost to the country as a whole and to most Americans, indeed to the world, with repercussions that persist today, the complexity engineered by the financial sector obscured the true state of affairs in the subprime mortgage area and led to the 2008 financial crisis and the Great Recession.

Our Short-Term Focus

Intrinsic to all the preceding developments has been an obsessive and counterproductive focus on short-term results, enabled by the growing sophistication of the computer. At the onset of the computer age, it was widely expected that the computer and associated technologies would boost productivity. Many find it puzzling that this never happened. Why didn't it? At least part of the answer is that the computer has been used more in service of instant gratification than long-term projects.

With the computer as a tool, investors and publicly traded corporations alike have become increasingly oriented toward the shorter term, seeking quicker results and profits. This parallels the short-term focus that took hold more generally in the United States in the aftermath of the 1971 snapping of the gold/dollar link.

One relevant statistic is stock turnover. Between 1949 and 1975, according to Ned Davis Research, investors held stocks for an average of about five years. True, one factor was that back then, commissions on the purchase or sale of shares were much higher than today. Since 1975, when stock commissions were allowed to fluctuate and then started to decline, turnover has been soaring, and average holding periods have taken a deep dive, down to about eight months.

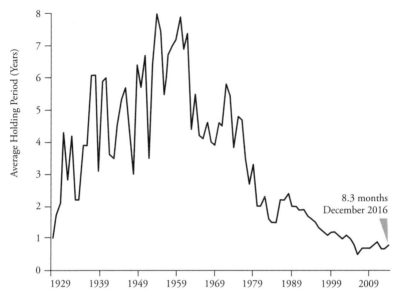

FIGURE 16.2   The decline in stock holding periods.
Source: Ned Davis Research, December 2016.

The only winners from high turnover are the wealth management and investment advisory firms that make up the core of the financial industry. But lower commissions are just a small part of the explanation. The entire focus of the financial services industry has shifted toward short-term results, starting with the obsessive attention paid to whether companies meet expectations for quarterly sales and earnings. If results for a company fall short, investors are quick to ditch a stock.

This contributes to the faster turnover. Even more significant, however, is the effect on how companies operate and make decisions, pressuring them to think in terms of the next quarter, not the next decade. After all, if investors bail out because of the latest quarter's figures, it will bring down the share price, which likely is tied to the compensation and bonuses of the company's executives. The need to meet expectations and to generate growth from quarter to quarter encourages companies to do whatever it takes to keep the party going, whether it's acquiring a rival or spinning off a division. Some of the time these might be smart moves that lay the groundwork for future growth. But often they are just attempts to keep shareholders happy.

The Onset of High-Frequency Trading

Warren Buffett is known to say his favorite holding period for a stock is "forever." The antithesis of Buffett's forever holding period is high-frequency trading (HFT). Embraced by Wall Street firms such as Goldman Sachs, HFT involves computers following complex algorithms to ceaselessly buy and sell shares in the space of nanoseconds with the goal of obtaining fractionally better prices on millions of trades a day for the traders' benefit. If you can come up with a plausible explanation for how this benefits the country and the economy, you're a lot smarter than I am.

HFT, made possible by nearly zero commission rates per trade, is perhaps the ultimate embodiment of our slide into short-term thinking. In his best-selling 2014 book *Flash Boys*, author Michael Lewis captures the sheer absurdity of it all. He describes the building of a $300 million underground cable linking the financial markets of Chicago and New York City. Its sole purpose was to give traders in New York data in 13 milliseconds (thousandths of a second) instead of in 17 milliseconds. Meanwhile, as economist Paul Krugman has pointed out, as this project was being completed, New Jersey Governor Chris Christie had just canceled a new rail tunnel under the Hudson River—one that, as NJ Transit riders who depend on trains to commute to jobs in New York City can attest, is desperately needed.

Yet another knock against the rise of the financial sector has been how it has siphoned off the best brains. In reviewing *Flash Boys* in the *London Review of Books*, John Lanchester commented: "I found it hard not to think about those missing oceanographers, the computer geniuses and engineers and physicists and entrepreneurs, all those brilliant minds, all that passion and energy disappearing into the black hole of money, lost to all the more productive and interesting things that we humans can do."

The point isn't that making money is immoral. It's that the way the system has developed this past half century in this country has exacted enormous costs and squandered opportunities. This helps explain why the United States now stands on the brink of being eclipsed by China as that country pursues its agenda of securing resources, creating infrastructure, and dethroning the dollar to create a new reserve currency tied to gold.

In the past, when the United States has really committed to a goal, we've accomplished big things. Today there is little understanding in this country of what our goals should be and of just how urgent the stakes are.

Before moving on, I want to make one more related point. It concerns long-term interest rates. Today in the United States along with many other Western countries, real low-term rates (nominal rates minus inflation) are near zero or even, astoundingly, negative. (Moreover, it is possible that real rates in the United States are even lower than they appear if, as I discuss in Chapter 18, the CPI understates actual inflation.)

Why does this matter? It's because the willingness of investors to accept such a low return from long-term bonds, whether issued by the government or by corporations, shows that at some level investors understand that opportunities for meaningful growth—growth that adds to productivity—are largely absent. The putative drivers of economic growth, namely the financial and technology sectors, contribute nothing meaningful and in fact, as I discuss earlier, likely make a negative contribution. Particularly problematic to productive growth is the combination of finance and technology dubbed *fintech*

At the same time, the persistently ultra-low interest rates are a natural ally of gold. The traditional knock against buying gold is that you're foregoing the opportunity to earn some return on your money. When real interest rates are zero or worse, that argument falls by the wayside.

17

The Toll of Rising Inequality

ONE OF MY earliest memories is of my grandfather extolling the virtues of America. The youngest in an immigrant family and a successful self-made businessman, he often said that one of the great things about this country was that everyone used the same products. His favorite example was the Gillette razor. In those days, it provided the best shave available, and almost anyone could afford it. Rich or poor, banker or janitor, when it came to a shave, Gillette was your brand.

This was in the mid-1950s. Today, Gillette still makes popular razors. But now there also are far more expensive razors geared toward the rich. One popular model, made by Feather, costs nearly $200. The last time I checked, it was rated 4½ stars on Google, indicating that those who could afford it considered its advanced engineering well worth the price. Feather's top-of-the-line razor sells for $600. This is more than a week's salary for Americans in the bottom 90 percent for income.

It's a small but telling sign of the income inequality that has grown so glaring in the last half century and that contributes, in more ways than many realize, to the country's decline. It's not that the United

States used to be a perfectly equal society, Gillette razors notwithstanding. Far from it, especially for minorities. Rich Americans had bigger homes, drove bigger cars, belonged to country clubs.

But the gap between rich and poor was less vast and less insurmountable. Far more than today, the perks of money and success served more as aspirations for the next generation of Americans than as goals forever out of reach. There was more social and income mobility. Since then, deepening inequality has made it far harder to move up.

Statistic after statistic attests to how much more unequal the U.S. economy has become. To cite one example, real paychecks (after inflation) since the late 1970s have risen, on average, 3.5 percent per year for the top 1 percent compared with around 0.5 percent for the bottom 90 percent. In other words, if you're in the top 1 percent, you've seen your salary rise seven times faster than almost the entire rest of the country.

There's rich and then there's ultrarich. Another marker of inequality is that in line with the outsized growth of the financial sector, the ultrarich—those in the top 0.1 percent—receive well over half their income from investments rather than from wages. For those at median household income levels, around $58,000 a year, only around 10 percent of income comes from investments. Clearly, the wealth generated by the financial sector largely benefits only those at the very top.

Perhaps most striking is today's huge differential between what CEOs earn compared with their employees' pay. In 2017, CEOs of more than 30 companies were paid more than 1,000 times the median pay of their companies' workers. In the 1970s, the average ratio was 40:1.

As you'd expect, these enormous differentials in wages and investment income have multiplied disparities in wealth. Today, the three richest Americans have more wealth than the entire bottom 50 percent of the country.

How Inequality Hurts Society

Rising inequality in the United States is deplorable. But is it really relevant in the context of making a case for higher gold prices? Yes. In multiple ways, inequality diminishes the country as a whole, eating away at our ability to accomplish the kinds of things we used to be able to achieve.

Inequality leads to more Americans who can't afford a good education, limiting their potential contributions of talent and income. Inequality leaves more Americans suffering from ill-health, able to contribute less while burdening the healthcare system.

It's not coincidental that the United States, formerly the world's most inventive country, today produces fewer patents per capita than any other developed country. Not only do we produce fewer than Great Britain, France, and Germany—we produce about one-tenth the number of patents as Israel and roughly *one-fortieth* as many as Finland.

All this weakens us relative to China, easing the way for China to prevail in all the areas that will propel gold prices far higher. And yes, China, too, has its inequalities. But as I discuss in a moment, inequalities in China are becoming less pronounced, not more.

In looking at how inequalities affect societies, I draw heavily on seminal research by Richard Wilkinson and Kate Pickett presented in their two books, *The Spirit Level: Why Greater Equality Makes Societies Stronger* (Allen Lane, 2010) and *The Inner Level: How More Equal Societies Reduce Stress, Restore Sanity and Improve Everyone's Well-Being* (Bloomsbury Press, 2018).

A key finding was that inequalities reduce social trust. Social trust became recognized as an important concept in the middle of the last century. It measures whether people think that most other people can be trusted, and it turns out to bear heavily on the success of a country and an economy. It correlates with economic growth and affects everything from life expectancies to health outcomes to whether people are likely to pay their taxes.

Wilkinson and Pickett quote sociologist Robert Putnam, who noted that social trust in the United States was high in the first two postwar decades but then began to ebb. "Sometime around 1965–70 America reversed course and started becoming both less just economically and less well-connected socially and politically," Putnam wrote.

The authors cite other studies that show that diminishing social trust correlates strongly with less optimism and loss of a sense of control at *every* income level, not just among the economically disadvantaged.

Some of the most interesting studies come from Great Britain. During both world wars, material living standards in Great Britain fell sharply across the board, yet life expectancies among civilians increased dramatically, much faster than in peacetime.

Although the conventional view of Great Britain here in the United States has been that it is more class conscious than us, offering less upward mobility, this is not true today, if it ever was. By almost any measure, including income levels and educational attainment, Great Britain today is more egalitarian than the United States And at every income level, the British have better health outcomes than Americans, whether you're looking at heart disease, cancer, diabetes, or other killers.

In other words, comparing Great Britain's wealthiest stratum with America's shows that even the richest Americans are hurt by our country's ultrahigh level of inequality.

Inequality in China

It's fairly straightforward to compare inequality in the United States with that in other developed countries like Great Britain. A more relevant question, however, is how we stack up against China, which is somewhat trickier. You need to dig a little deeper to make sure that you're comparing apples with apples.

According to several broad measures, inequality in China roughly matches that in the United States, but the reasons for it are quite different. Even more important, it is moving in the opposite direction: inequality is rising in the United States but narrowing in China.

As a very large developing country, China faces two chief income divides. One is a gap between urban and rural. This gap, despite the rapid and massive migration to urban areas, is still much wider than in developed countries. Urban areas offer the bulk of industrial and high-tech jobs, which pay more than the farming-related occupations of rural areas.

A related gap is the one between the country's east, which is more urbanized, and its west, which is more rural. The east has developed much faster and is far richer, for reasons ranging from its proximity to other Asian countries to Beijing being the seat of the central government.

Although these gaps are real, also true is that every income level in China has participated in the country's dramatic growth, in contrast to the United States, where for decades most Americans have seen almost no income gains. Moreover, recent data show that China's urban-rural divide has been narrowing because rural incomes have risen 67-fold since 1981. Returning to China's east-west divide, China has taken dead aim at lifting incomes in its western regions, home to more than 400 million people, spending well over $1 trillion in the past several years on the effort.

Strikingly, in less than two generations, China's poverty rate has fallen from 88 percent to about 0.7 percent as economic growth has lifted some 850 million people out of poverty. In the United States, efforts to reduce poverty have stagnated. Most studies suggest the poverty rate hasn't changed since President Johnson's war on poverty in the 1960s.

Studies that compare countries in terms of social trust have found that China ranks near the top. Edelman, which by revenue is the world's largest public relations firm and which conducts surveys of social trust, reported in 2018 that China "rose to the top of the Trust Index . . . [and] saw the most significant increases in trust across all of the key institutions: government, media, NGOs [nongovernmental organizations] and business. . . . [The] results are unprecedented in the history of the study."

The UN Human Development Index (HDI) is a broad-based composite that factors in everything from education to gross national income (GNI) per capita to life expectancies to environmental considerations. Not surprisingly, China trails most developed countries, including the United States. Within its income category, though, its score has shown the greatest gains in the past decade as China has moved up seven places. The U.S. score over the same period has shown little change and has dropped five places relative to other developed countries. To note one finding, at the beginning of the new century, life expectancy for the Chinese trailed that for United States by five years. Today, the gap is just two years.

Moreover, as reported in a Reuters' article presenting the findings of a 2018 World Health Organization (WHO) study, China has overtaken the United States in healthy life expectancy at birth. That is, while Americans may live two years longer on average, Chinese citizens go through old age enjoying better health and fewer age-related problems than Americans.

In the United States, differences in life expectancy between the first income quintile and the fifth are about 10 years. In China, despite a comparable or likely greater income differential between urban and rural residents, life expectancy between the two groups differs by fewer than five years. China's higher levels of social trust likely are important in explaining this finding.

Educational Opportunities in the United States . . .

Beyond food, shelter, and safety, parents throughout the world long to give their children a good education. Education is seen everywhere as the gateway to a decent life, essential for getting a good job and raising a family.

Throughout the United States, parents strive to live in neighborhoods with the best public schools. Those with the means to do so sometimes go to extraordinary lengths to get their children into top private schools and colleges. The recent scandal of celebrities and corporate executives bribing college coaches and committing other sorts of fraud to get their children into prestigious universities is this impulse taken to bizarre extremes.

Education is so important to a vibrant society that it deserves particular attention. In the United States, one of the most disbeartening results of rising income inequality has been declining educational opportunities for most Americans because college costs have risen more sharply than the costs in almost any other area. This is happening as education is becoming ever more essential for obtaining any sort of financial security, creating a vicious circle.

One revealing insight comes from looking at how much Americans in the top income decile (the upper 10 percent) spend on education per year compared with spending in the next highest decile. Those in the top decile spend three and a half times more.

This gap far exceeds spending gaps in other areas. For example, spending in the top decile on housing is about 70 percent more than in the next-to-highest decile. That is, the spending differential for housing is one-fifth that for education. Whereas inequality is large across the board in the United States, it is largest in the area most important for our collective future—education.

The highest decile was the only one where spending on education increased faster than inflation in education. Seemingly, only people in the top 10 percent had enough income or savings to increase spending faster than the burgeoning cost of higher education.

I think that it's reasonable to assume that most parents will spend as much as they can afford to send their children to the best schools. The large gap between the ninth and top decile strongly implies that if you're below the top 10 percent income level, your chances of attending the best schools lessen sharply. The long-treasured "American dream," the belief that upward mobility is possible for anyone willing to sacrifice and work hard, has faded into our past.

This conclusion is supported when you look at savings associated with various deciles. The highest decile has median savings of a bit less than $160,000. This is roughly what it costs to send two children to four years of an in-state public university, assuming that the children don't live close enough to commute and have to pay room and board as well as tuition. Even within the top decile, those below the median will find in-state public universities to be a stretch, whereas out-of-state public schools and private colleges are further out of reach. Of course, many students take out loans, but the debt burden such an action saddles them with for many years is yet another manifestation of the wrenching inequality in the United States today.

. . . and in China

Unequal access to education exists in China as well. The gap between eastern and western China has been seen in higher admission rates for eastern urban students to China's best universities. But there's evidence that educational access in China has been improving rather than getting worse, contributing to overall improvements in educational measures.

ChinaPower is an organization funded largely by U.S.-based think tank the Center for Strategic and International Studies (CSIS). It has reported that over the past decade, the educational index (EI), a measure based largely on the number of years of schooling, has risen faster for China than for any other country, whether developed or undeveloped. For Shanghai and Beijing, both big cities in China's east, the index is now equal to the EI in Organisation for Economic Co-operation and Development (OECD) countries, where the average EI has been falling. *New York Times* columnist Nicholas Kristoff recently pointed out that China is adding one university a week. Many are in rural areas, where educational attainment has lagged.

One thing to realize about China is that its millennia-old civilization has long hewed to the ideals of meritocracy. The country's top universities are probably the most selective in the world, with admission rates lower than one per 1,000 applicants. This is far more selective than any Ivy League school, where admission rates of five in 100 are considered daunting. In China, though, admissions are largely based on merit, as represented by test scores.

Urban dwellers do have an edge getting into the top schools both because of proximity and because urban areas tend to attract the most highly qualified teachers. Still, throughout China, the first nine years of education are mandatory and paid for by the state. Moreover, according to the China Project and *China Daily*, from 2003 through

2018, the state raised spending on education more than 15-fold, from $53 billion to above $800 billion, with a good chunk of this massive increase going to rural schools.

Several statistics attest to China's progress in education, in both relative and absolute terms. According to Nextfuture.com, at the start of this century, China had about 1.5 million new enrollees in higher education institutions compared with a bit more than 2 million for the United States. By 2013, new enrollees in China were 7 million compared with 3 million for the United States. Perhaps even more significant in today's world, the ratio of China science, technology, engineering, and mathematics (STEM) graduates to U.S. STEM grads was 8:1 in 2013. It's expected to rise to 15:1 by 2030.

A Truly Striking Statistic

I can't end this chapter on inequality without presenting one additional study that truly stunned me when I recently came across it. It looked at life expectancy for Americans at various income levels, comparing Americans born in 1930 with Americans born in 1960. I'll give the findings for woman, which were especially striking.

Women in the bottom quintile for income—the lowest 20 percent—who were born in 1930 and who reached the age of 50 could look forward to living 32 more years, to 82. Women in the bottom income quintile born in 1960 who reached the age of 50 were expected to live only 28 more years, to 78.

In other words, comparing women in the same bottom income quintile, life expectancy for those born 30 years later had dropped by four years—despite all the medical advances that had been made, all the lifesaving equipment hospitals have, and all the new medications that have become available. All this was overwhelmed by an income inadequate to take advantage of these advances or to otherwise provide a life conducive to good health.

It isn't until you get to the third quintile that life expectancy for women who reached age 50 was the same whether they had been born in 1930 or 1960. It's the wealthy who have reaped the benefits of all the advances in healthcare. When you get to the top 20 percent of income, women born in 1960 who reached age 50 had a life expectancy of 92 years, compared with 86 years if born in 1930.

I noted earlier that income inequality has less impact on health in China than in the United States. This may give China an advantage in coping with a common demographic problem, a population that is aging. In the United States and elsewhere, a sharply growing number of retirees will need to be supported by a relatively small number of employed. In China, many more older people, thanks to their relatively good health, will be better able to defer retirement. This may help counteract the lingering effects of China's prior one-child policy.

18

The Impact of Hidden Inflation

AS INEQUALITY IN the United States has widened, most Americans increasingly have struggled to keep afloat. Making this effort even harder is something that hasn't gotten much attention. It's that inflation has risen more than the official Consumer Price Index (CPI) figures indicate and in ways that hit hardest at those with the least to spend.

In Chapter 16, I noted that after Paul Volcker conquered inflation back in the 1980s, inflation has remained low ever since, underpinning the second postwar bull market. And this is true—as long as you're looking at the CPI. But the CPI number doesn't tell the whole story. A look at how it's derived makes it clear why it's misleading, understating actual increases in the cost of living.

There are two reasons I'm spending time delving into the inflation numbers. One is because of how it exacts a hidden toll on most Americans, accentuating the sting of the inequality that hurts them and the country as a whole. The other is because of what it says about our economy as a whole. If inflation is actually higher than reported, a corollary would be that productivity has been overstated. This, in turn, suggests that the gross domestic product (GDP) of the United States is less than reported. And that would mean that even in dollar terms, not just purchasing power parity (PPP), China may be closer to us in economic size and catching up to us more quickly than is recognized, further bolstering the case for higher gold prices.

Understanding the CPI

The Bureau of Labor Statistics (BLS) reports the CPI once a month. On the surface, it is a precise measure, reported to two decimal places (which implies a third decimal to allow for rounding the second). But this seeming precision is misleading. It's really a patchwork of assumptions and guesses.

The CPI is calculated as a weighted average of a basket of goods and services that BLS statisticians deem representative of what the typical American household consumes. The index consists of a large number of subbaskets, such as one for education, one for dining out, one for eating in, and so on. Most of these baskets consist of more than one item.

This methodology immediately provides us with one clue to the CPI's weaknesses. The only way it could actually measure inflation, that is, accurately look at how prices have changed over time, would be if the items that make up the basket, as well as their weightings, never change. But that's not the case. The goods that go into the basket frequently change for various reasons, and when that happens, new weightings are assigned based on an attempt to estimate how similar the new goods are to the older goods they've replaced.

The weights assigned to the baskets and to the goods in the baskets are determined by surveying households. When one item is dropped and replaced by another, it represents a best-effort stab by the BLS to come up with something that makes sense. For example, suppose that corn shortages result in fewer cattle being bred and hence higher beef prices, leading consumers to cut back on beef as a protein source. The green shades at the BLS might adjust by dropping beef from the food basket and replacing it with pork or chicken.

This substitution of one form of protein for another might seem logical, but it's far from precise. For instance, if pork were selected, you'd have to adjust for the millions of people who don't eat it for religious reasons. Allergies to substituted items are another factor to take into account. Calibrating the weights of these items to come up with a consistent cost-of-living measure is far more complicated than it might seem.

Keeping the basket up to date becomes especially challenging when entire groups of new consumer products are introduced, with the radio, television, and personal computer all obvious examples. Decisions on how to incorporate any such new consumer technology clearly involves making philosophical choices and recognizing that whatever choice is made won't apply equally to all Americans.

Hedonic Adjustments

And this just taps the surface of the problems with the CPI. One particularly dubious practice involves something called *hedonic adjustments*, which come into play largely with respect to the fast-changing technology area. Hedonism, of course, refers to the pursuit of pleasure. With respect to the CPI, though, you could say that hedonic adjustments ultimately have inflicted a certain amount of pain on many consumers.

Hedonic adjustments attempt to take into account the rapid improvements in the quality of electronic consumer products, from computers to TVs to cell phones, and relate them to the cost of living. The basic idea is that if computers, for instance, have become twice as fast as they were a year or two earlier but haven't doubled in price, they should be considered to have come down in price because you're paying less per unit of computing power—even if you don't really need that faster computing power. One effect of this is to rein in the overall CPI.

Is this approach valid? Let's look in detail at an actual example of how the BLS treated two generations of TV sets. The following table

gives the relevant data for two TVs, the older item A, which was dis-
continued, and item B, which replaced it in the BLS's basket of goods.

Characteristics	Item A	Item B
Price	$250.00	$1,250.00
Features	27-Inch Picture	42-Inch Picture
	Cathode-Ray Tube	Plasma
	EDTV	HDTV
	S-Video Input	S-Video Input
Characteristics	Item A	Item B
Price	$1,345.02	$1,250.00
Features	42-Inch Picture	42-Inch Picture
	Plasma	Plasma
	HDTV	HDTV
	S-Video Input	S-Video Input
	Universal Remote	Universal Remote

The table requires a bit of explanation. The top five rows are
straightforward: they compare the various features of the old and new
models. Clearly, the new TV offers more appeal: a much bigger screen,
plasma technology that would provide a clearer picture, and so on. But
it's also a lot more expensive: $1,250 versus $250.

The second half of the table is less obvious. It attempts to answer
the question posed by hedonic adjustment: what would the old TV
be worth if it gained every feature needed to be on a par with the new
model? The answer the BLS came up with is $1,345.02.

In other words, by the BLS's lights, the actual new TV, item B,
which consumers can get for "only" $1,250—some 7 percent less than
$1,345.02 (love the precision of the two cents!)—is a bargain. And
somewhere in the BLS's calculations for the year, this will translate into
a 7 percent *decline* that will factor into the overall price of its home
entertainment basket.

Wow. There's so much you could say about this that it's hard to
know where to start. Maybe the fact that most jumps out is that you

could buy five of the old TVs for the price of one new model, and yet it's officially viewed as a price decline.

To many consumers, this won't seem like a decline. If you have a home with several TVs that you might want to replace but you also need to save money for your children's college education, the supposed 7 percent decline in price won't seem like such a bargain. Not so incidentally, education costs—one of the most troubling aspects of modern life for millions of Americans—don't have a large weighting in the CPI.

Or suppose that you're in your 20s with lots of college debt and renting a very small apartment with one TV that had cost you just $250. Suddenly a new model comes along whose higher quality supposedly reduces your TV entertainment costs by 7 percent. What are the odds, given that you're living in modest circumstances presumably because you can't afford anything better, that you could afford a $1,250 TV? Probably not high.

It is the same idea for computers and other electronic devices. It's true, as suggested earlier, that if the latest computer model has twice the power of the prior model but sells at the same price, you could look at it as a significant reduction in price. But this says nothing about whether the faster speed is meaningful to a particular user. It might mean a lot if you're running a hedge fund or in a rarefied area of scientific or mathematical research. For the typical consumer, however, the only area where raw speed really makes a difference is in playing video games. If you use your computer for emailing and for browsing the internet and composing the great American novel in your spare time, the increased power of your computer's chips will mean little.

Hedonic adjustments are a dicey attempt to give a dollar value to technological improvements. Their overall effect has been to understate rises in the cost of living. Because the CPI is used as the basis for such things as computing adjustments to Social Security payments, it has contributed to keeping wages and Social Security income lower for many lower-income Americans, precisely the ones who are hardest hit by the actual rise in living costs that the CPI helps conceal.

Meanwhile, hedonic adjustments and the technologies they apply to might make sense for one group of individuals—those who are extremely wealthy and who would have no problem replacing their TVs with a passel of TVs costing many times more. Hedonic cost-of-living adjustments may not be the major villain when it comes to income inequality, but they play a role.

Housing Costs

Looking at how the BLS deals with housing also is informative. Housing makes up the largest single weighting in the CPI, at around 41 percent. It includes three subbaskets: shelter (32 percent of the overall CPI), fuels and utilities (5.1 percent of the CPI), and household furnishings and operations (4.4 percent).

The shelter subbasket has four components: rent for a primary residence (5.9 percent of the CPI), lodging away from home (0.8 percent), owner's equivalent rent (24.9 percent), and tenant and household insurance (4 percent).

None of these baskets and components made it into the CPI until 1983. Until then, the index factored in housing simply by considering the price of an apartment or a home. In 1983, the BLS brought into play the notion of *equivalent rent*. To calculate it, the BLS asks homeowners how much they think they'd have to pay to rent their home. Renters who are surveyed are asked what they pay in rent.

One problem with this methodology is that the homeowners' answers are necessarily based largely on guesswork. As for renters, no distinction is made between tenants in rent-controlled and rent-stabilized apartments and those paying market-based rents. Nor is a distinction made between tenants who have occupied the same apartment for a long time—which keeps rents down—and those who have rented more recently.

Financial writer Wolf Richter has pointed out that the BLS could have chosen instead to use *market rents*, a common measure of the actual rents negotiated by prospective tenants with landlords. Market rents would give a more accurate picture of the rents would-be tenants are encountering in real time. Richter calculates that between 2011 and 2014, market rents rose 12.1 percent, whereas owner-equivalent rents rose just 4 percent. In other words, this is another example of how the BLS's approach has led to the CPI understating rises in the cost of living.

The understatement is even greater when you compare owner-equivalent rent with the Standard and Poor's (S&P)/Case-Shiller Home Price Index. Starting in 1999, home prices rose faster and higher than owner-equivalent rent. Even after the housing bubble burst in 2009 and residential real estate prices dropped between 30 and 50 percent, they remained above renter's-equivalent rent.

Productivity and GDP

How does this all tie in with productivity and GDP? A hypothetical example shows the connection. Suppose that the BLS replaces steak with chicken because chicken prices have dropped relative to steak prices. Now suppose that research shows that ounce for ounce, steak has more protein and a healthier mix of nutritional chemicals than chicken. This would mean that the new basket would offer lower nutritional value than the preceding one.

This would mean that for a family to maintain a constant level of nutrition, it would have to pay more, either by buying more ounces of chicken per meal or by springing for the more expensive steak. In terms of nutritional costs, inflation has risen rather than remaining constant, as the two supposedly equivalent baskets would imply.

Productivity enters into the picture because when consumers need to buy and eat more chicken to obtain the same nutritional benefits, it will take additional person-hours to produce the extra ounces of chicken required. But the BLS doesn't take those extra person-hours into account. As a result, it understates the number of person-hours needed to produce comparable amounts of nutrition. And that's another way of saying that it is overstating productivity.

If this is not clear, look at it this way. Suppose that it takes one person-hour to produce a pound of chicken and one and a half person-hours to produce a pound of steak. If you don't consider nutritional value, you'd conclude that the new basket, with chicken, takes fewer person-hours to produce and that therefore productivity has risen. However, if the new basket is in fact inferior, the supposed gain in productivity is bogus.

The hedonic example of the two TVs is another example of how, depending on the assumptions you make, the impact on productivity might be negative rather than positive and inflation higher than reported. That hedonic adjustment, you'll remember, allowed a TV that was less than one-fourth the price of a newer model be valued as more expensive because it lacked some high-tech features. But if, as I argued, those new features are worth a lot less money to many consumers than the hedonic adjustment implies, inflation would be understated, productivity overstated, and real GDP overstated as well.

The Service Sector

It gets even trickier when you try to assess inflation and productivity in the service sector, including in the financial area. With manufacturing, at least you can be guided by the idea that more is better: Producing more of the same or a very similar thing in fewer person-hours means that productivity has gone up. With services, it's not always the case that more is better.

For instance, remember those financial advisers who rake in big fees providing advice that leaves investors worse off than if they had simply invested in passive indexes? Can you really argue that more advisers providing more bad advice raises productivity? Similarly, most studies show that stock investors who make fewer trades do better than those who trade more often. If this is the case, then does the ability conferred by the computer to make more trades really add to economic productivity? The same questions apply to all the new financial products that have been developed. Though some may add to overall financial well-being, others brought on the Great Recession.

There are no easy answers. According to the Bureau of Economic Analysis, however, the average financial employee accounts for nearly half a million dollars of national income, whereas, in aggregate, what is counted as financial income—profits plus compensation—constitutes 17.5 percent of overall national income. I'd argue that some of this, rather than being counted as financial income, should be counted as inflation, extra money paid to financial workers for accomplishing nothing and in some cases less than nothing.

The bottom line is that you can make a strong case that national income is being overstated. And because with a few technical adjustments national income equates to GDP, it means that U.S. GDP has been overstated as well.

Comparisons with China

If U.S. GDP is actually smaller than reported, there's a definite irony in that. The conventional wisdom has long been that China's figures can't be trusted and that China exaggerates the size of its economy. Of course, both countries could be reporting figures that err on the high side. If anything, though, the most comprehensive and peer-reviewed studies strongly suggest that China actually understates its economic size.

For example, in 2015, the Center for Strategic and International Studies (CSIS) sponsored a study that addressed the real size of China, titled "An Independent Look at China's Economic Size." The authors are two well-respected researchers associated with the Rhodium Group and its extensive studies of China. They concluded that through 2013, China's dollar GDP was understated by more than 10 percent.

The main reason for the understatement related to the service sector and, in particular, to activities related to real estate. The CSIS/Rhodium study was published in 2015, a year in which the Chinese experienced a great deal of turmoil in their financial markets, including a devaluation of the yuan. These events once again bring up the possibility of Chinese understatement of GDP, especially when China reported that the fourth-quarter GDP was greater than 6 percent.

A separate study came from the National Bureau of Economic Research (NBER). The authors, Hunter Clark, Maxim Pinkovskiy, and Xavier Sala-i-Martin, are affiliated with the New York Federal Reserve Bank and Columbia University. The paper's title, "China's GDP Growth May Be Understated," gives away only part of the conclusion. The abstract sums up both the conclusion and the prevailing wisdom at the time: "Our computations of Chinese growth based on optimal weightings of various combinations of economic indicators provide evidence against the hypothesis that the Chinese economy contracted precipitously in late 2015, and are consistent with the rate of Chinese growth being higher than is reported in the official statistics."

How much higher? The authors' estimate was a range of 7 to 10.6 percent compared with the reported 6.7 percent.

These may all seem like somewhat academic concerns, but economic size counts. In particular, it has a lot to do with a country's influence when it comes to the world's monetary system and reserve currency. China already has the edge when it comes to trade because it is indisputably the world's biggest trader. As I noted earlier, its military strengths are formidable, more than sufficient to defend what it sees as the country's vital interests. If in terms of economic size it is approaching the United States even when measured in dollar terms, this could augur a revamped monetary system, one linked to gold, happening sooner rather than later.

19

Sputnik Moments
Then and Now

SPUTNIK MOMENT IS a well-worn catchphrase that continues to resonate. It signifies a rude awakening and a commensurate rising to the occasion. This is a sequence the United States sorely needs today.

The original *Sputnik* moment came in the 1950s when the Soviet Union's successful launch of the *Sputnik* satellite forced the United States to confront the shocking revelation that the Soviet Union had leapfrogged us in space technologies. It was a wake-up call, and it woke us up. The United States responded by allocating billions of dollars to science, technology, engineering, and mathematics (STEM) education and massive research and development (R&D) efforts that, in little more than a decade, culminated in our being first to land a man on the moon.

Sputnik has been on my mind lately. One reason has been the effort by the U.S. government to throttle China's leading technology company, Huawei. And no, this is not what I'd call a *Sputnik* moment–like response—quite the opposite. But it does raise the question of what today's genuine *Sputnik* challenge is and how we should meet it.

First, Huawei. It's a remarkable company that is widely acknowledged as the leader in the technologies that will form the basis of 5G mobile networks. Its products are technologically superior to as well as less expensive than anything produced by Western companies and have won global acclaim. Rather than react by building up our own capabilities, the United States has simply tried to kick the Chinese company out of the game. Our actions are the same as if in the 1950s, rather than ramp up STEM efforts, we had simply shot *Sputnik* out of the sky.

We've banned Huawei products in the United States (with the temporary exemption of rural telecoms) and ordered U.S. chipmakers Intel and Micron, among others, to stop selling chips to Huawei. As justification, the United States has cited Huawei's potential to be a conduit of Chinese spying, and pushing that narrative, we've pressured our allies around the world to shun Huawei products in their own wireless 5G networks. Australia has sided with us. European countries, however, seem skeptical of U.S. arguments that Huawei is a security threat, and developing countries are almost certain to embrace Huawei's offerings.

There's good reason for skepticism about the U.S. claims. There has never been hard and fast evidence that Huawei has used its equipment to spy or that its equipment contains the backdoors that would make spying possible. In fact, unlike any other telecom company, it has provided source code, enabling prospective customers, including governments, to examine in detail the software that manages Huawei products. So far at least, nothing in the code suggests a backdoor.

But still, what's so wrong with taking a strong stand against Huawei if there's even a remote chance that it's a security threat or just to push back at China, which is challenging us on so many fronts? The answer is that it's a shortsighted approach that is likely to backfire, both with respect to Huawei specifically and for our overall interactions with China.

If we don't knock out Huawei entirely, and I think the odds of doing so are so low as to be virtually nonexistent, the company will emerge stronger than ever, with such a commanding lead that it won't need to work with U.S. companies at all. This would be broadly harmful to U.S. tech companies. Right now, the United States leads in chip design. By denying U.S.-made chips to Huawei, we're forcing it to catch up in the one tech area where the United States still can claim a lead. I think that Huawei will be more than up to the task, not only of catching up but of eventually surpassing us and other leading players.

After all, this is what Huawei has done with 5G, where its major competitors aren't U.S. companies but rather the Scandinavian companies Erickson and Nokia. Huawei's superiority in 5G is why so many countries still want to use Huawei products despite U.S. pressure. Countries that blackball Huawei in 5G are settling for an inferior mobile network as the foundation of crucial tech areas—from the Internet of Things to artificial intelligence.

More recently the United States has extended its ban on technology exports to other Chinese companies. The bans encompass a broad array of items, including not just processors but also interconnectors and highly specialized chips.

The Supercomputer Race

It's important to be aware of the full scope of China's tech capabilities, which extend well beyond Huawei. I referred earlier to China's lead in hypersonic missiles, which has made the country virtually immune to military attack. Supercomputers, perhaps the pinnacle of information technology, constitute another high-tech area where China has demonstrated an impressive ability to catch up and then some.

Supercomputers are defined empirically as the 500 fastest computers in the world. At the century's start, China had only two supercomputers in this elite group, and neither one was high up in the rankings.

By 2010, China and the United States were just about equal in the number of their supercomputers in the top 500—and one of China's was ranked number one as the very fastest. China's supercomputers were built from off-the-shelf parts, including processors made by Intel. After several years of China being number one, the United States banned exports of Intel's fastest chips to China. This proved a self-defeating strategy: within a year, China had created a new computer that not only was even faster than its former model but also was built with processors designed and made entirely by China.

China still dominates the top-500 list with more than 200 machines—nearly twice as many as the United States has. However, for now, the United States has the two fastest machines.

China aims to reclaim the number one spot, but this time using chips and components made solely in China. The next generation of supercomputers will likely be introduced within the next year or two. Known as *exascale computers*, they will be able to perform at least a billion billion calculations per second. The United States will probably introduce them first. China likely could beat the United States to the punch but has said that it will hold off until it can build the exascale computer with parts made exclusively by China.

China is looking even farther ahead as well, to the 2030s, when it expects to have readied a generation of supercomputers 1,000 times faster than exascale machines and, again, made entirely from Chinese parts.

Win-Win or Lose-Lose

In other words, China has shown that it can more than hold its own in any technology race with the United States. This no doubt irks the heck out of the United States, but I think that for China, the purely competitive aspect is of secondary importance, tangential to its real concerns. This is because I don't see China as viewing the world today as simply a new iteration of the 1950s and 1960s, in which two big powers vie for dominance. Or, to put it differently, China doesn't see things as a zero-sum game.

Rather, I believe, China appreciates that today's true *Sputnik* challenge isn't a matter of one country beating another. Instead, it's the urgent need to beat the existential challenges posed to every country by coming resource scarcities and the pressures they will put on the world, if not addressed in time. Cooperation among countries, not conflict, makes success that would benefit everyone more likely. If it's not win-win, it will be lose-lose, with everyone suffering.

This perspective likely helps explain why China reacted less strongly than it could have to U.S. technology bans. China could have retaliated, for instance, as some thought it might, by embargoing exports of rare earth metals to the United States, disrupting virtually all our most sophisticated technologies. Or it could have crippled, if not destroyed, U.S. companies such as Qualcomm, for which China is far and away the most important market.

Had China raised the stakes in such a manner, geopolitical disputes now being fought along economic lines risked escalating into a much more dangerous military clash. And while China may feel confident that it could defend itself, it may have calculated that there was nothing to gain by closing the door to potential U.S.-China cooperation on a range of mutually important issues.

Resource Scarcities, Again

If the United States could see today's *Sputnik* moment more as I believe China does, we'd be better off. Resource scarcities along with climate change make it imperative to prepare for coming times with an all-out, not-a-moment-to-waste effort to make optimal use of resources to create renewable energy infrastructure. It's a truly pressing challenge because the planet today is nearing a civilization-threatening juncture. So far, however, we're still slumbering. Far from being rudely awakened to the new reality, we've resisted recognizing it. We continue to take resources for granted. And we seem, for now at least, increasingly committed to viewing our relationship with China as a zero-sum game.

I've already discussed many of the interrelated factors that will lead to resource scarcities, and I've tied them to coming explosive gains in gold prices. But this is such an important challenge, above and beyond its investment implications, that I want to return to it here with some additional data. My major source for the figures presented herein is the World Bank.

One reason for complacency in the United States has been a tendency to focus narrowly on data that misleadingly support a rosier outlook. Recently, for instance, some analysts have been citing data that seemingly suggest that the world uses fewer resources today to grow than it did in the past.

In one sense, this is true. In most countries, including the United States and China, resources as a percentage of GDP have been falling. Good news, it would seem. But when you look more closely, the data provide no reassurance that we're winning the fight against resource scarcity for the simple reason that global GDP is growing faster than the percentage of resources per unit of GDP is declining.

Some 2.5 percent of China's GDP in 2000, for example, consisted of natural resources, including fossil fuels, forest products, and agricultural land. By 2017, the last year for which there's data, the figure had dropped to 1.5 percent. But China's population was bigger and so was China's GDP, with growth in both outstripping the decline in resource use per unit of GDP.

This is like trying to argue that a house built in 2017 that is 3 percent copper must use less copper than a house built in 2000 that is 5 percent copper and that therefore housing overall in 2017 consumes less copper. This is true only if you assume two things: the houses are the same size and the same number of houses are being built. But what if houses in 2017 are bigger and more are being built? It's irrelevant that copper is being used more efficiently: the bottom line is that a lot more copper is being consumed.

Some additional figures, also from the World Bank, help round out the picture. In 2017, the world's per-capita consumption of resources in dollars had more than doubled, and so had the world's per-capita income. (The conclusions would be nearly the same if we used purchasing power parity [PPP] instead of dollars.) This means that resource efficiency has enabled incomes to grow at the same pace as population growth but has not allowed per-capita GDP to grow faster than resource consumption.

The problem is that for 85 percent of the world, per-capita GDP is below $5,000. For the remaining 15 percent, it's above $40,000. In the United States, it's above $60,000. The ratio in resource use between the haves and have-nots, therefore, is more than 8:1.

For some perspectives, poverty in the United States is considered to be a per-capita income of about $13,000. This means that globally, for the have-nots to reach a per-capita income level equivalent to *poverty* in the United States, resource consumption would have to nearly triple. For the rest of the world to move up to the *average* of the world's haves, resource consumption would have to climb about eightfold.

More recent data show that between 2015 and today, resources as a percentage of GDP have been increasing in much of the world, possibly because it takes more resources to produce resources. Whatever the explanation, it is evidence that unless something changes, the push by the great majority of the world's population to obtain a decent standard of living will be thwarted. The consequences are likely to include rising levels of unrest, all-out revolutions, and wars.

The Compelling Message

One compelling message is that we should waste far less time and effort developing technologies that are essentially frivolous and focus instead on ones that can solve civilization-threatening problems. China has seized this mantle, acquiring the biggest technological lead in areas relating to the use of resources.

By a wide margin, China dominates solar and wind energies. It also has developed techniques for improving infrastructure productivity that leave the rest of the world in the dust. To give one example, China recently announced completion of one of the world's largest airports, a multibillion-dollar infrastructure project completed months earlier than scheduled and within its initial budget. Germany is building a major airport that already is nine years behind schedule and whose current estimated cost is three times the original.

Virtual reality and augmented reality are examples of technologies that improve infrastructure construction. They allow engineers to fully realize detailed measurements and visuals of a finished product before construction has begun. According to the well-regarded website Foreign Policy, American investments in these technologies were $120 million in 2018. China spent nearly $4 billion. Moreover, the Chinese were far and away the leading exporter of these tools, which enhance the critical job of building out infrastructure.

These examples give a hint of where we should be focusing our efforts, both by developing our own capabilities and by cooperating with China so that we can avail ourselves of its best technologies. Trying to "win" by crippling China is the very epitome of suicidal shortsighted behavior. Taking a long-term view and seeking ways and areas where we can fruitfully work together, to everyone's benefit, would be rising to the occasion in a way that future generations will be grateful for.

Meanwhile, whether we act wisely or not, gold prices will soar. The chapters that follow take you into the myriad ways you can invest in gold, from coins to funds to individual miners of all sizes. As with all investments, there are tradeoffs between potential risks and rewards, and some diversification among the different choices is always a good idea. Regardless of *how* you choose to invest in gold, however, don't pass up the chance to get in on what I believe will be a truly once-in-a-lifetime opportunity.

20
Investing in Gold, Part 1: Physical Gold

WE HAVE FINALLY come to our endpoint: investing in gold. As the forces described in the preceding chapters emerge with ever greater clarity, gold prices will rise, and rise some more, and then rise some more, albeit, I have no doubt, with dips along the way. Investors should start to stake out positions in gold now, with a view toward accumulating more over time.

When it comes to investing in gold, there's good news and bad news. The good news is that you have a lot of choices. The bad news? You have a lot of choices!

You can buy gold bars. You can buy gold coins. You can buy antique coins. You can invest in a gold fund. You can buy shares in a big-cap miner that's already producing gold. You can buy shares in small gold companies that have yet to mine an ounce. It's all wide open, and especially if you're new to gold investing, this can be daunting.

As gold prices double and triple and more in coming years, a lot of money will be made in all the preceding possibilities. But there are pros and cons to each. In this final section of this book, I'll walk you through the opportunities and drawbacks as best I can. The truth is that there's no one right way to invest in gold, though I feel that there are a couple of wrong ways or, at least, ways I wouldn't recommend.

There are three broad categories to consider: physical gold, individual gold mining companies, and funds—and each contains subcategories. In this chapter, I look at the ins and outs of physical gold.

Bars, Rounds, and Coins

A while ago, I had a rather memorable conversation with the manager of the precious metals portion of a major state's pension fund. He was bullish on gold and said that he'd bought shares in a gold exchange-traded fund (ETF) for his client. I asked him if he owned it himself as well, and he said, hell no. For his own gold investing, he said, he bought gold bars—the actual physical stuff.

A lot of gold enthusiasts feel the same way—that nothing beats actually owning physical gold, or bullion. Are they right? In many ways, you can't argue with them. Owning physical gold has a lot of merit and will be a surefire—and in some respects the safest—way to benefit from gold's coming gains. However, it also has some undeniable hassles and isn't for everyone. To help you decide if it is or isn't right for you, here are some of the basics.

The first thing to realize is that even if you like the idea of owning physical gold, you still have more choices to make. Physical gold comes in different forms: bars, coins, and rounds. Coins are further subdivided into the collectible/numismatic type and contemporary coins.

All these forms of gold come in various weights and dimensions and are produced by mints and refiners around the world and sold by dealers. One important distinction is between mints and refiners. Mints are either fully or partly government owned. They are the only entities officially authorized to produce coins that are recognized as legal tender.

These coins have a face value, but their actual value is far greater because of the intrinsic value of the gold that constitutes them. The best-known mints include the U.S. Mint, the Royal Canadian Mint, the Perth Mint, and the South African Mint. The most popular coins are the American Eagle, the Canadian Maple Leaf, and the South African Krugerrand.

Refiners produce bars and rounds (both of which mints can produce as well) but not coins. Rounds are similar in appearance to coins. But they aren't recognized as legal tender because they are issued by private refiners that do not have a relationship with a government. Popular refiners include PAMP Suisse, Englehard, and Credit Suisse.

Prices of all these forms of physical gold are determined by the spot price, which is derived from the Comex futures market and the London Gold Fix. All bullion products rise and fall in value in accordance with fluctuations in the spot prices. The products sell at a premium to the spot price, with the spread typically narrowing during bear markets in gold and widening when gold prices are trending upward.

Coins normally sell at a premium to bars. The spread in price between the two usually widens when gold prices are trending upward and narrows when gold is trending downward. A few years ago, when gold was correcting, the difference between a one-ounce gold bar produced by the Royal Canadian Mint and a one-ounce Maple Leaf coin was $10. The difference was more than $100 dollars in 2011 when gold hit a peak.

Older coins tend to cost more than more recent ones. In addition, coins issued in certain years or with special designs may be more valuable than standard coins from the most recent year.

Choosing between coins and bars depends in part on what quantity of gold you're looking to buy. Most coins come in weights of one ounce or less, whereas bars range in size from 1 gram to 400 ounces. Because you pay a premium for buying coins, buying a large bar lets you get the most gold possible at the lowest cost. As an illustration, if the spread between coins and bars is $50 per ounce and you want to buy 10 ounces of gold, you'd pay $500 more just to get that gold in the form of coins rather than in a bar.

But coins have some advantages over bars. If you're looking to buy just a small amount of gold at a time—a fraction of an ounce—they'd be a natural choice. In addition, it may be easier to sell coins if you need to cash in. With bars, you may have to offer proof of their purity. Some dealers may require that you pay to have the bars fire assayed, meaning melted down so as to validate that they reach the requisite level of purity. Or potential buyers may test them by newer methods, such as x-ray scanning, ultrasound, or acid testing.

You can avoid having to worry about proving purity if you buy bars that come in a sealed plastic security case with a serial number and/or an assay certificate containing a barcode. Look for bars that state that they are "In assay." In general, there's no issue if you stick with bars that are no more than 10 ounces in weight and that are manufactured by one of the major mints. And the path is even smoother if you sell the bar back to the dealer from which you had bought it (make sure that you keep the receipt).

If you're new to gold buying but like the thought of owning physical gold, I suggest that the most straightforward approach is to stick with coins produced by a reputable mint and not look for what might seem like better deals from other sellers. It's worth paying the premium to be assured that you're getting what you think.

I see no reason not to simply start with the U.S. Mint, which is the major source of gold coins in the United States. Each year it produces more than enough gold coins to satisfy investor demand. The U.S. Mint assays the coins it produces; all its coins are 24 karat and are sold to qualified dealers, who then sell to gold investors. The dealers may charge a premium as much as 8 percent above gold's price, partly reflecting the hefty premium they pay to the U.S. Mint. But you still may be getting a decent deal, especially if the dealer offers services such as storage. For a list of qualified dealers, visit https://catalog.usmint. gov/bullion-dealer-locator.

In any case, when you buy physical gold in any form, you need to find a safe place to store it, and under your mattress isn't a real option, though an in-home safe or vault is a possibility. So is a safe deposit box or private storage facility and vault. You also should buy insurance. These are all unavoidable tasks and expenses that go along with physical gold.

There's no doubt that when it comes to both buying and selling it, physical gold is a more cumbersome and time-consuming process than the other forms of gold investing that I'll be covering, which basically involve nothing more arduous than picking up a phone or opening your computer. So why bother with physical gold? After all, when you want to have a stake in most other kinds of assets, you invest in shares on paper. If I think the food production sector will be strong, I buy shares in Deere Co.; I don't buy a dozen tractors and then have to find a place to park them.

But gold is a special case. With most other investments, there's an implicit assumption that the system will hold. A particular company might always fail, or there could be a steep economic decline, but in the end, you're investing with the notion that the world as you know it will remain intact and that things will bounce back.

You can invest in gold in the same spirit. This, in essence, is my perspective. It's true that the case I make for gold's rise rests on my view that the world is changing in profound ways. But I'm not anticipating a doomsday implosion. I'm not urging you to run for the hills.

Traditionally, though, many investors in gold are motivated by a belief or fear that maybe the center won't hold. In buying gold, they are looking to hold insurance against total economic mayhem. Under these circumstances, only physical gold will suffice to stand up to the general chaos. Owning gold on paper might provide no greater protection than owning shares in companies that have gone belly up.

Again, I want to stress that I'm not predicting such chaos and don't expect it. I'm just pointing out that if you're inclined to worry that doomsday is lurking in the shadows, physical gold makes a lot of sense. It can't fail, it can't go bankrupt, and it will be the asset that will get you through the direst of times.

21
Investing in Gold, Part 2: The Miners

THIS IS NOT hype. Honestly. In a major bull market in gold, if you invest in the right mining companies, you can ultimately make 40 to 50 times your money. Maybe even more. Of course, there are no guarantees. You might make "only" 20 times your initial investment in one mine or overall. And some mines might run into problems and turn out to be poor investments.

When it comes to investing in gold, I admit that my personal preference runs to focusing on miners. The best-situated miners offer the greatest leverage to gold's gains. They're easy to buy. Some even pay a dividend. You have a range of choices, from the more speculative junior miners to large-cap companies with a proven record of production. Even if you want to own physical gold, I'd suggest investing in some miners as well.

The key, of course, is to pick the right miners and to be sufficiently diversified among them so that if one or two don't pan out, you still win big. Identifying the right miners isn't a matter of luck. There are sensible guidelines for evaluating miners of all sizes for both safety and potential. I've screened dozens of mining company and in this chapter present the ones that have made the cut and that I expect will be among the stars as gold's price rises.

Before moving onto the guidelines and specific companies, though, I need to stress that there are no guarantees or promises. As with any investment, things can change rapidly. When recommendations appear in a book that won't be read until months after it's written, it's especially important to remain mindful of that reality. In my investment publications I can switch gears rapidly as facts dictate, but a book doesn't offer the same flexibility. So as you read through these investment chapters, keep in mind that the investments I highlight represent my best thinking at the present time but should not be taken as etched in stone.

Now for those guidelines and most promising miners.

An essential rule when evaluating mining companies is to have knowledge of, and confidence in, the experience, knowledge, and integrity of their leaders. This is important in any investment, of course, but it's particularly critical with miners, because so much of what will determine their success is, literally, concealed deep underground. Above all, I look for miners whose bosses have great long-term records in the industry.

A second guideline is to focus on miners operating in geopolitically safe regions, keeping them shielded from chaos or threats of government expropriation. This narrows the field, but—with an occasional exception—it's not worth incurring the risks of investing in regions that are particularly vulnerable to violence or other types of disruption. Of course, to some extent, this is a moving target. Chile, for instance, is blessed with resources and, until recently, was considered one of the most politically stable countries in South America. But the large-scale protests that have recently erupted there have modified this calculus.

In the end, with miners as with any investment, you're weighing risks against potential rewards. In the case of the mining stocks I present herein, the potential rewards range from big to megabig, whereas the risks are well measured and well worth taking. I've divided the companies into three categories: junior miners, mid-cap miners, and large-cap miners. I'd strongly recommend diversifying both across and within these categories. I also present two exchange-traded funds (ETFs) that track gold miners: one for the junior miners and one for larger-cap miners. These offer another way to participate as gold prices rise and mining stocks come into their own.

Junior Miners

The gold investments with the biggest potential rewards are the small mining companies known as *junior miners*. These are companies that own or have significant stakes in properties known to contain gold and often other precious metals but that haven't yet started mining operations. Many are still in the midst of the long and multistage process of obtaining the necessary environmental permits, an inescapable task for any miner. Because they are not yet generating earnings, they may need to seek funding to keep the process going, to build the necessary infrastructure, and to conduct exploratory operations to determine the likely potential of their holdings.

Even though investing in junior miners seems to require a certain degree of faith, the key is to make sure that it's not blind faith. Some junior miners will fall by the wayside, but the ones that make it will reward you many times over, greatly leveraging the rise in gold itself. I can't eliminate all the risks, but I've done the legwork to single out the junior miners that are the most solidly situated while offering potential rewards that are among the highest you will find in any investment area.

These are companies in which you can make multiples of your initial investment in a gold bull market as they go from money-losing companies to producers, in some cases achieving the ranks of major producers. To cut the risk, I have focused almost exclusively—with one attractive exception—on miners with assets in politically safe regions. Even at current gold prices, each would be profitable shortly after beginning mining operations because the costs of production, at below $1,000 per ounce, are far lower than what they'd get for their gold sales.

NovaGold

If I had to pick just one junior miner to recommend, NovaGold Resources would be the clear choice. It's likely the world's largest junior miner, and once it has developed, it will become one of the world's largest miners. Its major property, the Donlin mine, in terms of measured reserves and resources is likely the largest undeveloped gold deposit in the world.

Donlin is located in southwest Alaska within the Kuskokwim Gold Belt. The Kuskokwim has been producing gold since the end of the nineteenth century. Through 1959, most of that gold came from what is known as *placer mining*, which involves gathering up gold that lies on the surface of streambeds or at the bottoms of streams.

Placer mining is a simple process that can be carried out by a single prospector. Remarkably, between 1908 and 1959, approximately 600,000 ounces of gold were found in the region simply by sifting through sand and streambeds. This is a clear sign of how rich in gold the area is, with vast amounts almost certain to be found once modern mining methods come into play.

Donlin's current mineable resources are pegged at nearly 40 million ounces of gold. This figure is likely to expand by many multiples once more aggressive exploration gets going and defines additional resources. Donlin is in a remote part of the state, far from Alaska's major cities and infrastructure, which has limited exploration so far. However, once the necessary infrastructure is built and the mine is up and running, exploration will proceed full bore.

In developing Donlin, NovaGold has a heavyweight partner, Barrick Gold Corp. (GOLD), one of the world's largest miners. The two companies are 50/50 partners in Donlin. The partnership began in 2007 and has been mainly devoted to exploration and to satisfying the strict environmental rules that govern mining in largely pristine areas.

As of this writing, almost all the necessary permits have been granted. This lets the companies move on to obtain the financing they need to build the multibillion-dollar infrastructure that will support mining operations.

Based on current estimates of mineable gold, and with gold at its current price of about $1,500 an ounce, NovaGold's net present value (NPV), which includes capital expenditures, is $5.8 billion. (NPV is a metric that attempts to calculate the ultimate value of all the minerals that will be mined.) This is approximately 2.5 times the current capitalization of the stock.

At gold's current price, there are other junior miners that, because they are further along in exploration of their holdings and have less capital development ahead of them, have higher potential return multiples of NPV than NovaGold does. None of them, however, have the kind of upside potential that NovaGold has if we get the full-fledged gold bull market I anticipate. This potential is driven by the inherent leverage NovaGold has to higher gold prices, which comes from its ability to sharply ramp up gold production once the infrastructure is in place. For example, at a gold price of $2,500, NovaGold's NPV rises to more than $13.5 billion, which is more than six times the company's current capitalization. At a gold price of $5,000, the potential return would be close to 14-fold.

This is just the start. Beyond leverage to the price of gold from quickly starting to produce its known reserves, NovaGold likely has even greater leverage to the additional gold reserves and possibly other minerals that will be defined at Donlin. It's often the case in the mining industry that even in areas that are well explored, reserve estimates are only a small fraction of what eventually gets mined. The more that gold's price rises, making it economically feasible to go after more locations and grades of ore, the more this holds true. And for NovaGold, as I said, a lot of exploration lies ahead.

John Dorba is a retired University of Nevada professor. He notes that gold reserve estimates for Nevada, probably the most prolific gold-producing state of the 48 contiguous states, have climbed eight-fold since 1990. In Donlin, where relatively little exploration has been done, reserve estimates could easily multiply by 10-fold or greater as more geologists start working out growth plans with NovaGold management.

Over the next decade or so, could you make 100 times your money in NovaGold? Maybe not. But I can tell you that I hate asking stupid questions, and from everything I see, this is far from a stupid question.

NovaGold has one other positive that for me emphatically seals the deal. Its biggest shareholder, with a 26 percent stake, is Electrum Strategic Resources, a private holding company focused on gold and, through another holding company, Triology Metals, on other minerals such as copper and cobalt. Electrum is controlled by Tom Kaplan, whom I consider to be one of the most knowledgeable, shrewd, and successful gold investors of our time. The fact that he sees NovaGold as one of the most promising gold mining companies in the world and has put his own money into it is a meaningful endorsement

Tom also happens to be a long-time personal friend. His interest in gold and other precious metals preceded mine, and I've benefited from his extensive knowledge and experience. My belief that gold is headed for a massive bull market stems from my own analysis of all the geopolitical trends presented in these chapters. Tom, who earned a B.A., M.A., and Ph.D. in history at Oxford, brings a broad historical perspective to his view that gold's ascent this decade will be inevitable.

During the market crash of 2008–2009, Tom was buying small gold stocks. His one public investment in gold has been a relatively small gold mine that he started buying in 2009 and continued buying through 2012. During this period, while gold itself performed well, most gold stocks struggled—but as of this writing, the one gold stock Tom owns on which there is public information shows him with a double-digit profit.

But Tom isn't all about money. To the extent that the public knows of him, it's because of his lifelong passion for big cats. His nonprofit organization Panthera, the leading organization dedicated to saving snow leopards and other big cats in the wild, has been featured on *60 Minutes*. Tom also has a passion for Flemish art and owns the largest private collection of Rembrandts in the world. I see both these pursuits as perfect complements to what animates him as an investor—to pursue his passions and focus on the enduring.

Gabriel Resources

Another junior miner with exceptional potential is Gabriel Resources (GBRRF). This is a different sort of wager than with NovaGold. With Gabriel, it will be all or nothing. If its gold mine gets developed, you can count on enormous rewards. But development of the mine could get blocked, in which case you'll be out of pocket. Right now, as I write this, the shares are so cheap that I think it is definitely worth a shot as a portion of your gold holdings for any investor with a speculative bent.

Headquartered in Canada, Gabriel has as its major asset a gold mine in western Romania that is the largest undeveloped mine in Europe. The company has been caught in a political tug of war between an environmental group headed by George Soros on one side and pretty much everyone else with an interest in the outcome. The jury is still out on which side will prevail, but the winds now seem to be blowing in the direction of the mine coming online.

Romania is the poorest country in the European Union, and development of the mine would lift the country's GDP by a meaningful amount. The last NPV analysis was done in 2014 when gold was trading below $1,300. At that time, the mine's long-term value—the NPV—was estimated to be about $1.6 billion, or roughly 6.5 times the current value. With gold at $1,500, the figure would likely be above $10 billion. And with gold flying high in a bull market, Gabriel easily could be a "30-bagger."

One positive sign for the mine is that Gabriel just completed a $25 million private placement that suggests that investors both longtime and new have not given up on the mine after fighting Soros for about a decade. It's also worth paying attention to who is investing in the mine. Top holders of shares include Baupost Group, a private investment partnership headed by Seth Klarman, whom many consider the top long/short investor of his time. His 20-plus-year record is one of the best in the hedge fund world. Tom Kaplan's Electrum is another major holder. So is Newmont Goldcorp, a large-cap gold mining company that I recommend later.

International Tower Hills

International Tower Hills (THM) is a Canada-based junior miner whose major asset is the Livengood Mine, located near Fairbanks, Alaska. It obviously passes the test of location in a stable jurisdiction, and it has the added benefit of ready access to infrastructure.

This is one of the most leveraged gold mining companies around, and as gold's price rises, the stock price should rise far more. Since early 2016, the shares have risen some 200 percent as gold has gained 35 percent. The rise in gold boosted the company's after-tax NPV from negative $500 million to about $250 million. The stock sells at a discount to NPV because the company still has to obtain additional permits.

All of the company's board members have at least 25 years of experience in Alaskan mining and know the ins and outs of operating in the state. It's not anticipated that the company will run into problems obtaining the remaining permits.

The leverage is enormous. If gold goes back to its previous highs of $1,900 an ounce, investors easily could value the stock at $1 billion or more. This implies a nearly 10-fold gain from the current price. Moreover, history shows that in gold bull markets, investors value future earnings even more than current earnings for a first-class gold miner. This suggests that a long-term gain of 30-fold would be within reach.

If gold rises to $2,500 an ounce, which is well below what I expect it ultimately to achieve, the potential gain would be between 25- and 50-fold. Electrum has a substantial stake in the shares. Two other big holders of shares are John Paulson, of the Paulson hedge fund, and Tocqueville Asset Management, which in addition to managing private funds also runs the very successful Tocqueville Gold Fund, an open-ended mutual fund dedicated to gold.

Medium-Sized Producing Mines

Now I come to the middle of the pack, miners that are neither big nor small. But this doesn't mean boring or mediocre. I've singled out two midsized producing miners. Both have established strong track records in every metric that counts, from increased production to rising reserves to earnings. One even pays a dividend

Although their potential gains are likely less spectacular than for the juniors, each has a well-measured long-term target. At a minimum, I am targeting each to double, and they are likely to do considerably better. Both have strong balance sheets, so even if gold were to back off to $1,000 an ounce, they'd still have enough cash to continue to generate growth in their reserves and resources. For investors, these medium-sized producers offer a nice tradeoff—less speculative than the juniors but more upside potential than the majors.

Endeavour Mining Corp.

Endeavour Mining Corp. (EDVMF) is headquartered in Australia and operates mines in Western Africa. And yes, at first blush, Africa might not seem to meet my criterion of a politically stable locale. But Western Africa is a part of the continent that has been less subject to turmoil.

Eight West African states operate under the auspices of one central bank and use a common currency pegged to the euro. Economic policies are aligned and monitored by the International Monetary Fund. Royalty payments to countries for mining are relatively constant across countries.

The region is largely made up of democracies. Indeed, all eight states had an election in the past decade. Burkina Faso and Cote d' Ivoire—two of the three countries where Endeavour has mines—had elections in 2015 and have elections scheduled for 2020. The third country where Endeavour operates, the Republic of Mali, had an election in 2018.

Western Africa has been growing at a breakneck pace, by more than 80 percent over the past 15 years. During that time, the region has become one of the world's top gold mining areas. Production in 2018 likely exceeded 9 million ounces, leaving the area in a battle for second place with major gold producers Australia and Russia, behind first-place China.

In another sign of the region's importance in gold, between 2006 and 2016, West African gold mines have raised $6 billion in equity, more than Australia and second only to Canada. Nearly 80 million ounces of gold have been discovered over the same period, making the region by a sizable margin the world's most fertile.

Among midsized miners operating in West Africa, Endeavour stands out for consistently beating expectations for production and for new mining discoveries. In 2019, for the first time, all four of its major mines have been producing. Results so far have exceeded projections, with gold production rising at a solid and sustainable rate.

Continued growth in production is positioning the company for a breakout both in profits and in free cash flow (free cash is the money a company has left over after all expenditures, including capital investments). Endeavour will be able to use its growing free cash flow to reduce debt and continue what has been a highly successful exploration program.

With gold at $1,500, estimates of mineable gold approach 25 million ounces. Even if gold, contrary to what I expect, remains in a trading range for the foreseeable future, the company is deeply undervalued. A steadily rising gold price will lead to a many-fold gain in the share price.

Fresnillo

Now for something a little different. The second midsized mine I am recommending is Britain-based Fresnillo PLC (FNLPF). What sets it apart from my other picks is that it produces a lot of silver along with gold, giving me a chance to comment on investing in silver as the gold bull market accelerates.

In coming years, silver is the one commodity likely to give gold a run for its money. Silver's history as a monetary metal and store of value extends even further back than gold's. Some 4,000 years ago, in ancient Greece, it became the first metal to be used in trade. Since then, silver coins have often been legal tender, and countries, including the United States, have used silver to back paper money.

Silver has a lot in common with gold but is less rare and more easily tarnished. It's also less dense. This bears on silver's suitability as a monetary metal because it means that silver takes up more space than gold, a consideration when it comes to storage. The ratio is about 2:1, meaning that an ounce of silver requires twice as much room as an ounce of gold. Although this ratio is far less than the relative values of the metals—as of this writing, an ounce of gold is worth 80 times an ounce of silver—it's enough to put gold into a different class as a monetary metal.

And often being just a little bit better translates into a dramatic differential in value. A nose better in a horserace can bring millions more dollars in stud fees. When investors focus on monetary issues, gold can get an enormous premium over silver, as is the case today.

Silver also differs from gold in having important industrial uses. It's the world's best thermal and electric conductor and plays a key role in areas ranging from medicine, in killing bacteria, for example, to solar energy. This industrial role, where silver often has no ready substitutes, works against it as a monetary metal relative to gold because it means that some silver gets destroyed. In contrast, gold—whose few industrial uses can be easily performed by other metals—does not get used up. It's thought that almost every ounce of gold that has been mined still exists on the face of the Earth. Being fixed in quantity is exactly what you want in a monetary metal

All this said, silver will continue to be seen as a store of value and to be prized in jewelry. And its simultaneous leverage to monetary inflation and industrial demand makes silver unique. When gold prices are rising, silver prices often rise faster—especially if industrial scarcities come into focus. By contrast, when gold corrects, silver tends to fall more. Since mid-1975, when the first postwar gold bull market really took off, gold has more than doubled silver's performance. However, when gold was rising, silver was the only metal to come close to gold's gains and at times even exceeded them.

All of this is to say that it would be a nice addition to have a solid stake in silver. Fresnillo offers a way to get it on the cheap.

Headquartered in London, it has mines in Mexico that make it the world's largest silver producer. Silver accounts for around 35 percent of its overall production. Gold—it's Mexico's largest gold producer— accounts for a bit more than 50 percent, and lead and zinc account for the remainder.

At its current level as I write this, the company offers investors a spectacular buying opportunity. The shares fell sharply in mid-2019 when the company reported that projects to boost production at two of its seven mines were taking longer to complete than expected. As a result, production, rather than increasing, fell by around 10 percent. By October, the stock had dropped nearly 30 percent for the year against gains of about 30 percent for the average mine. This massive divergence moved the stock from one of the largest capitalized mines to a mid-cap with a valuation of about $6 billon.

But while the delays in the growth projects were disappointing, investors' reactions speak more to their focus on the short term than to anything more problematic. The company has a strong record of delivering solid gains in production, and its longer-term prospects remain intact.

The company attributes the delay in its growth projects to infrastructure issues that should be resolved by the end of 2020. That, along with other projects, should position it to generate growth in production and in proven and probable reserves through the next decade.

A third project, Juanicipio, which will be classified as a new mine, is also scheduled for completion by the end of 2020. This alone should make up for the shortfall in 2019. The completion of all three projects by yearend 2020 should translate into record gold and silver production.

Some analysts argue that Fresnillo's valuation metrics are still relatively high, even after the drop in the shares. But this overlooks the long-term growth prospects, attributable resource base, and leading position in silver.

At the end of 2018, Fresnillo had attributable resources of 2.2 billion ounces of silver and 39.1 million ounces of gold. These assets, which correlate strongly with long-term production prospects, put Fresnillo in the same class as mines with valuations several times higher. Moreover, these numbers don't take into account the many additional exploratory opportunities for the company not only in Mexico but also in Peru and Chile.

In a bull market in gold and silver, this first-class producing miner offers potential gains that nearly match those of many well-positioned junior mines. Over the next decade, a tenfold gain would not be a surprise.

Big-Cap Miners

For the greatest leverage to rising gold prices, the junior miners are your ticket. But there's nothing wrong with owning large-cap, more established miners, either instead of the juniors, depending on how aggressive an investor you are, or alongside them. As with everything, there are tradeoffs.

Leverage to rising gold prices comes from the ability to increase production, and the juniors, by definition, will be increasing production because they are starting from no production. The bigger-caps will struggle to raise production and may actually see production start to decline. Still, as gold prices rise, the gold they continue to produce will bring in more money and generate rising profits. And because of their larger size, the bigger mining companies offer greater safety in the event of some out-of-the-blue catastrophic event.

The three large-cap gold stocks that I recommend here should have no trouble keeping up with the metal and very likely will solidly outperform it while significantly outperforming the stock market.

Newmont and Barrick

Newmont (NEM) and Barrick (GOLD) are the two heavyweight gold miners. You won't go wrong with either, but of the two, I prefer Newmont. This is especially true for investors who own shares in

NovaGold. Because of Barrick's 50 percent interest in NovaGold's Donlin mine, picking Newmont over Barrick diversifies your portfolio more than by owning Barrick and NovaGold.

Newmont's recent merger with Canada's Goldcorp will translate into a roughly 43 percent jump in gold production, to nearly 7.5 million ounces a year. The company should be able to maintain production at this level until the middle of the decade. Rising production will be complemented by declining costs.

To sustain production at this level, Newmont will need to develop additional assets. Given that Newmont has the highest capital budget in the industry and a history of generating high returns, there's reason to be confident that it will succeed. The company's debt is nearly equaled by its cash, whereas free cash flow should reach around $1.8 billion by the early 2020s. While I can't promise that Newmont will be leveraged to the gains in gold, of the major miners, it has far and away the best chance.

This isn't to say that Barrick is a bad company to own. Far from it. I recommended Barrick in my newsletter when it became clear that then-CEO John Thornton was up to the task of reducing the company's bulging debt. Over the past several years, company debt has been reduced from more than three times earnings before interest, taxes, depreciation, and amortization (EBITDA) to less than twice EBITDA. However, gold production has declined fairly sharply during this period.

In 2018, Barrick merged with Randgold, and Randgold's head, Mark Bristow, took over as Barrick's CEO. Bristow has an exceptional record of bringing new mines up to snuff quickly and without hitches. Still, with worldwide growth in gold production slowing and maybe even close to peaking, he faces a daunting task. Although slowing production growth is another reason to be bullish on gold, it makes it hard for the major gold producers to move the needle when it comes to production. And without higher production, it is very difficult for a mine, however well managed, to be leveraged to rising gold prices.

One of Barrick's best shots at raising production comes from its highly productive mines in Nevada. Newmont, however, has a more than 30 percent interest in those mines through its joint venture with Barrick. So, if you buy Newmont, you are gaining a stake in one of Barrick's prime properties.

In other words, to the extent that Barrick does well, Newmont and NovaGold should do considerably better in toto. That Newmont's assets are more geographically secure means that a potentially bigger payday comes with less risk.

Franco-Nevada

Franco-Nevada (FNV) has a very different business model from the preceding two large-cap gold miners. In fact, it's not a miner at all: it's a streaming and royalty company with about 85 percent of its operations in gold and precious metals and more than 10 percent in oil and gas. In essence, it acts as a financier for startup resource companies and also provides additional capital for ongoing operations.

In exchange for investing cash in startups, Franco-Nevada generally receives future royalties in the form of a percentage of top-line revenues. Another source of revenue comes from streaming, where Franco-Nevada pays a miner a fixed price for a secondary metal. For example, silver is often a by-product of zinc mining, so Franco-Nevada might pay a zinc miner for the right to buy future silver production at an agreed-upon price. Franco-Nevada also sometimes pays for a working interest in the mines of an operating company.

Royalties and streaming dominate the company's revenues. Because royalties have no ongoing costs and streaming has just a fixed cost per ounce, these revenue streams are far more profitable—more than 100 percent, on average—than a working interest in a mine.

The company's business model results in high leverage to rising commodity prices with almost none of the risks of higher capital costs associated with mining. And the model works across a very diverse set of assets. The company currently has stakes in more than 375 assets spread around the globe. Virtually all of them are in politically stable countries, including the more than 80 percent in the Americas.

The company's oil and gas assets are focused in the extremely fertile Permian and Scoop/Stack basins in Texas and Oklahoma. Note that even if I'm right in my contention that fracking ultimately can't ward off oil scarcities, production from fracking will be substantial for a while longer, benefiting Franco-Nevada.

Since the company's initial public offering in 2008, most operating measures such as revenues, EBITDA, and gross profits have grown by five- to sevenfold. Earnings per share have grown more slowly because some of the funding for projects has come from the issuance of additional shares. Dividends, however, have grown at a 17 percent annualized rate and should top $1.00 per share next year.

Since going public, the company has generated about $4 billion in EBITDA, the broadest measure of earnings. Going forward, current operating projects promise an additional $20 billion of EBITDA. And this does not include returns on an additional 230 gold, silver, and other metal projects and nearly 60 oil and gas projects, all in the startup phase, with meaningful production set to start over the course of the decade. Add to this any additional investments the company makes, and you have a rare combination of the potential for explosive growth with limited downside risk.

Since 2008, Franco-Nevada has outperformed other gold investments—mines and physical gold—by a wide margin. This reflects the explosive growth in its royalty, streaming, and various ownership relationships over a wide range of mines, along with its more recent royalty arrangements with shale oil companies.

For the five-year stretch 2019–2023, organic revenue growth should exceed 35 percent, which is much higher than for any other major gold company. Moreover, the vast bulk of these revenues will come without the risks typically associated with gold mines, including accidents and injuries.

Over the next five and more years, Franco-Nevada will increasingly reap the benefits of its past investments as they start to mature. As a result, free cash flow, which turned positive in 2019, is likely to grow nearly fourfold through 2023, when it will approximate $900 million. With its pristine balance sheet, the company will be free to use this excess cash to invest in new opportunities and to raise dividends. Despite gold's volatility since 2008, Franco-Nevada has raised its dividend every year. Going forward, there should be less need to issue additional shares to fund investments, which should translate into faster dividend growth. This is icing on the cake, as the shares expand many times over this decade.

22

Investing in Gold, Part 3: Funds

FOR MANY INVESTORS, the simplest way to get in on gold's rise will be to invest in a fund. This is fine, but you need to know which ones are good choices and which to avoid.

Here I look at three types of funds: exchange-traded funds (ETFs) that track the price of gold, ETFs that track the miners, and mutual funds. And I offer some general investing principles, related to margin and leverage, that can help you avoid a lot of grief.

Bullion ETFs

ETFs burst on the scene in 1993 and, understandably, quickly became a huge hit with the investing public. They are designed to simply track an index—a stock index such as the Standard and Poor's 500 Index (S&P 500), an index of a particular market sector such as defense stocks or precious metals—any slice of any market anyone might want a stake in. EFTs have a lot of advantages. They trade like stocks, making them simple to buy and sell. Their fees are generally lower than those of mutual funds. They also are easier at tax time because taxes are owed only when you sell the ETF. With mutual funds, your taxes are calculated based on every trade a fund manager makes of stocks in the fund's portfolio. Finally, in terms of performance, passively managed ETFs that mirror stock indexes such as the S&P 500 by and large have outperformed most money managers as well as actively managed mutual funds.

Investing in an ETF that tracks gold bullion lets you participate in gold's rise without the hassles of buying and storing physical gold. The following figure lists four ETFs that track gold's price, comparing their performance during various periods over a 10-year stretch through mid-February 2020.

Symbol	ETF Name	1 Year	3 Year	5 Year	10 Year
GLD	SPDR Gold Shares	22.3	23.0	42.2	−10.0
IAU	iShares Gold Trust	23.4	23.5	43.1	−8.8
SGOL	Aberdeen Physical Swiss Gold	23.6	22.8	42.7	−12.6
BAR	GraniteShares Gold Trust	23.5	N/A	N/A	N/A

FIGURE 22.1   Four gold bullion ETFs.

The differences among the funds are minor, related primarily to fees and different levels of liquidity. iShares Gold Trust (IAU) has lower fees, which explains why it has outperformed the other three. But it holds less gold and is less liquid than SPDR Gold Shares (GLD), though that won't affect most investors. GLD is the largest and best-known gold ETF and is often considered a proxy for gold. One advantage to GLD's larger size is that it might be better able to survive any sort of crisis—malfeasance, fraud, theft. But both IAU and GLD are very suitable vehicles for long-term investments in gold.

Switzerland-based Aberdeen Physical Swiss Gold (SGOL), with its gold held in Switzerland, on average, has slightly underperformed GLD and IAU because of its somewhat higher fees. These fees, however, have reflected the Swiss franc's strength vis-à-vis the dollar, and because the dollar has strengthened this past year, SGOL has outperformed others. GraniteShares Gold Trust (BAR) is a relatively new ETF whose gold is stored in London, meaning that its relative performance improves when the British pound underperforms the dollar.

I consider any of these ETFs to be a perfectly acceptable—and certainly easier—alternative to owning physical gold. But you should be aware of one distinction—that between *allocated* and *nonallocated* gold. One advantage to owning physical gold is that it's allocated—you are the sole owner of the specific bars or coins you've bought.

This is not true when you invest in an ETF. Ownership of the gold that the ETF holds to back up its shares is divided among all the stakeholders in the fund, and if anything goes wrong with the fund, there's no assurance that you can reclaim your portion. I would not worry much about this, but it's just something to be aware of.

Mining ETFs

Other ETFs track the performance of indexes of mining stocks. If you prefer not to pick and choose among the various miners presented in Chapter 21, or if you feel that you wouldn't be able to diversify among them enough, mining ETFs offer an alternative way to gain a stake in gold. Remember, I expect that as the bull market in gold unfolds, the biggest gains will be made not in gold itself—awesome as those gains are likely to be—but in mining companies leveraged to gold's price. So I think that it would be a shame not to put at least some of the money you are allocating to gold into miners, either directly or via a mining ETF.

The following figure lists five mining ETFs. The best known are VanEck Vectors Gold Miners ETF, with the stock symbol GDX, and VanEck Vectors Junior Gold Miners ETF, which trades under the symbol GDXJ.

		Major Gold ETFs			
Symbol	ETF Name	1 Year	3 Year	5 Year	Gold High 8/22/11*
GDX	VanEck Vectors Gold Miners ETF	33.80	27.00	53.70	–46.70
GDXJ	VanEck Vectors Junior Gold Miners	33.40	11.30	84.10	–63.40
GOEX	Global X Gold Explorers	20.80	6.10	98.30	–62.10
RING	iShares MSCI Global Gold Miners ETF	42.20	27.40	58.60	–31.40
SDGM	Sprott Gold Miners ETF	22.80	21.70	43.00	N/A

FIGURE 22.2 Five mining ETFs.

GDX tracks 45 gold stocks including the major miners. Because it is weighted according to capitalization, the biggest miners count most. The three biggest—Newmont Goldcorp, Barrick, and Franco-Nevada—together account for roughly 30 percent of the ETF. Although you can gain greater diversification with GDX, my preference still is to buy Newmont Goldcorp and Franco-Nevada individually. But GDX is certainly a decent proxy for a stake in the senior miners.

GDXJ tracks junior miners, including some small miners that already have begun some production. Some of my favorite miners, such as NovaGold and Endeavour, do not have a large weighting. So I think that you might reap bigger gains by buying the individual mines, but again, you do gain diversification with the ETF.

A lesser-known ETF is Global X Gold Explorers (GOEX), which defines itself as following an index of gold explorers, smaller-cap miners that are similar to the junior miners and that in some cases may overlap with them. This fund is the most volatile: it has the strongest five-year performance but has lagged over the past one- and three-year periods. Also, despite sharply outperforming the senior miners over five years, it has underperformed them over the past eight plus years because of the correction in the 2011–2015 period.

iShares MSCI Global Gold Miners ETF (RING), like GDX, is largely devoted to senior gold miners but follows an index that is the most diversified across geographies. So far this diversification has paid off; the caveat is that this ETF was not around for most of the 2011–2015 correction.

Finally, Sprott Gold Miners ETF (SDGM) is a collection of gold stocks chosen by analysts rather than one that follows an index. Since its inception, it has lagged, providing another example in which active management underperforms simply following an index. Still, Sprott analysts are top notch, and the ETF could surprise in a long-lasting bull market.

Shun ETNs

A subcategory of ETFs should be strictly avoided. Known as *exchange-traded notes* (ETNs), some try to tempt investors by promising to leverage returns. But the risks on the downside vastly outweigh the potential gains on the upside. Unless you are an experienced short-term trader with money to spare, don't go near them.

Like ETFs, ETNs are designed to follow particular indexes. But instead of owning the underlying investments, an ETN buys a security from a bank, with the price based on the value of the index. This adds an extra element of risk pertaining to the creditworthiness of the bank issuing the note: if the bank goes bankrupt, you're out of luck.

Also problematic is that ETNs are relatively opaque. Invesco DB Gold Fund (DGL), for instance, is an ETN intended to give investors a stake in the price of gold. Rather than follow gold's price directly, however, it follows futures on gold. This makes it more speculative, dependent on the level of interest rates and other factors, and its returns aren't easily explained by changes in gold's price.

The biggest problem is with ETNs that promise to leverage your returns. The idea is that if the underlying index goes up, the ETN goes up more. The problem is that if the index goes down, your ETN dives more steeply.

Consider the two gold mining ETNs in the following figure. Direxion Daily Gold Miners Bull 3X (NUGT) represents senior miners, whereas Direxion Daily Junior Gold Miners 3X (JNUG) represents junior miners.

		Selected Gold ETNs			
Symbol	ETF Name	1 Year	3 Year	5 Year	Gold High 8/22/11*
NUGT	Direxion Daily Gold Miners Bull 3X	74.70	−18.80	−65.30	−96.00
JNUG	Direxion Daily Junior Gold Miners Index Bull 3X	55.50	−56.30	−64.30	−96.00

FIGURE 22.3   Two ETNs.

The *3X* in the names conveys that whenever the index rises by any amount on a given day, the ETN will triple that gain. For instance, if you own NUGT and the group of senior miners on which it's based rises 4 percent on any one day, the ETN rises 12 percent. If the group falls 4 percent, the ETN falls 12 percent.

You might reason that if the overall trend for gold and stocks is up, it might pay to take a chance. After all, if the ETN goes up more days than it goes down, why worry about the down days?

The reason is a pesky inherent asymmetry between up and down moves in any investment—and that is magnified when gains and losses are leveraged. This is a really important principle worth taking the time to understand.

The idea is that a move up—say of 4 percent—isn't the same as a 4 percent move down. And when this asymmetry is multiplied by three, any significant drop in an investment results in a very steep hill to climb just to get back to even.

Suppose that you buy one of the preceding leveraged ETNs at 100 and then it drops 7 percent for three consecutive days. On day 1, its value declines to 79. By day 3, you will have lost a bit more than 50 percent.

Now suppose that on the next three days the index rises 7 percent a day, meaning that you gain 21 percent each day. You should be fine, right? Not so fast. When you do the math, over that six-day period you'll have lost about 12 percent—your initial 100 is now worth only around 88. What would have happened if you had bought the same index without leverage? At the end of the six days, your investment would be worth roughly 98.5.

This is a huge differential. The lesson is that with a leveraged ETN, any big drop can leave you permanently in the hole. The real-world results for the two ETNs in the figure show that this isn't just a theoretical concern. Whereas both showed gains over the past one-year period, they were in the hole for three years and deep in the whole for five years—down around 65 percent. By contrast, all the plain-vanilla mining ETFs showed strong gains in all time periods, including total gains ranging from roughly 43 to 98 percent over the past five-year stretch.

The leveraged ETNs are a disaster for anyone seeking long-term gains in gold. I view them as another example of how the financial industry gets individuals to pony up fees for the privilege of losing money—and in this case, it can be a near-total wipeout.

Buying on Margin

Speaking of leverage, I offer comparable advice—that is, avoid it—to investors tempted to buy gold ETFs on margin, something ETFs permit. With margin, you can invest as little as 50 percent of the ETF's value and double your gains if gold goes up. Of course, as with the ETNs, if gold goes down, you're out of luck. *Plus*, you pay interest on your margin.

If you don't trust me on this, then trust Warren Buffett, who has advised investors not to buy his stock, Berkshire Hathaway, on margin. Despite Berkshire's extraordinary past success and Buffett's confidence in the company's long-term prospects, he knows that at times Berkshire has declined as much as 50 percent from a previous high.

If you had owned Berkshire on margin during one of those declines, you could have lost your entire investment and then some, because brokerage houses insist that investors, for safety reasons, continue to add to their investment as the stock drops.

Even more galling, you might have been wiped out just at the moment when you could have jumped on a great buying opportunity. One of the declines came toward the end of the wild early 1999–early 2000 bull market in tech stocks. In the wake of that crash, Berkshire soared.

The second 50 percent decline in Berkshire occurred during the 2008–2009 bear market. Again, a fully margined investor would have lost out on a major comeback.

My view is that gold is headed dramatically higher, indeed dramatically higher, because of a seismic shift in the world's financial underpinnings. But I don't see any reason to take unnecessary chances when you can make so much money in gold just by playing it safe.

Mutual Funds

In addition to ETFs and ETNs, there also are mutual funds dedicated to gold, mainly by owning a collection of mining stocks. Mutual funds are actively managed and by and large perform less well than ETFs while charging higher fees.

In general, therefore, I don't see any particular reason to choose a gold mutual fund. Just to cover all the bases, I'll mention one possible exception: First Eagle Gold Fund (FEGOX), simply because it holds both a collection of gold miners plus gold bullion. However, while this might be a convenient one-stop choice, over both the past 10- and 5-year periods, you would have done better by investing half of your gold-allocated money in a bullion ETF and the other half into an ETF of large gold miners.

Wrapping Up

I started this book's investment section by saying that the good news and the bad news about investing in gold are that you have a lot of choices. You now probably understand what I meant. But the really good news is that whichever route you take among the investments I've commented favorably on, you should end up happy campers.

The even better news is that the bull market in gold, although it may suffer temporary pullbacks, won't be a short-lived affair. Over what is generally considered the longer term, five years or so, I anticipate that gold could rise three- to fivefold. But I expect that gold's uptrend will persist far longer than five years and go far higher. It's more likely to be several decades before gold tops out at many multiples of its current price. Gold is the essential investment of these and of coming times, setting you and your family up for life in a world that will be changing in dramatic ways.

Further Reading

Allison, Graham, *Destined for War*, Houghton Mifflin Harcourt, Boston, 2017.

Beiser, Vince, *The World in a Grain*, Riverhead Books, New York, 2018.

Bell, Daniel A., *The China Model*, Princeton University Press, Princeton, NJ, 2015.

Coyle, Diane, *GDP*, Princeton University Press, Princeton, NJ, 2014.

Denton, Michael, *The Wonder of Water*, Discovery Institute Press, Seattle, WA, 2017.

Ellis, Chris Devonshire, *China's New Economic Silk Road*, Asia Briefing, Kowloon, Hong Kong, 2015.

French, Howard W., *Everything under the Heavens*, Alfred A. Knopf, New York, 2017.

Gordon, Robert J., *The Rise and Fall of American Growth*, Princeton University Press, Princeton, NJ, 2016.

Hall, Charles A. S., and Klitgaard, Kent A., *Energy and the Wealth of Nations*, Springer, New York, 2012.

Hessler, Peter, *River Town*, HarperCollins, New York, 2001.

Inman, Mason, *The Oracle of Oil*, W.W. Norton & Co., New York, 2016.

Jacques, Martin, *When China Rules the World*, Penguin Press, New York, 2009.

Jastram, Roy W., *The Golden Constant*, Edward Elgar Publishing, Cheltenham, UK, 1977 (reprinted by World Gold Council, London, 2009).

Johnson, Ian, *The Souls of China*, Pantheon Books, New York, 2017.

Keay, John, *A History of China*, Basic Books, New York, 2009.

Khanna, Parac, *The Future Is Asian*, Simon & Schuster, New York, 2019.

Kwarteng, Kwasi, *War and Gold*, PublicAffairs, New York, 2014.

Kynge, James, *China Shakes the World*, Houghton Mifflin, Boston, 2006.

Lardy, Nicholas R., *Markets over Mao*, Peterson Institute for International Economics, Washington, DC, 2014.

Latiff, Robert H., *Future War*, Alfred A. Knopf, New York, 2017.

Lee, Kai-Fu, *AI SuperPowers*, Houghton Mifflin Harcourt, Boston, 2018.

McAfee, Andrew, *More from Less*, Scribner, New York, 2019.

McMahon, Dinny, *China's Great Wall of Debt*, Houghton Mifflin Harcourt, Boston, 2018.

Maloney, Michael, *Guide to Investing in Gold and Silver*, Wealth Cycles, Scottsdale, AZ, 2015.

Mead, Walter Russell, *God and Gold*, Alfred A. Knopf, New York, 2008.

Nikiforuk, Andrew, *Slick Water*, Greystone Books, Vancouver, Canada, 2015.

Prasad, Eswar S., *Gaining Currency*, Oxford University Press, Oxford, UK, 2017.

Scheidel, Walter, *The Great Leveler*, Princeton University Press, Princeton, NJ, 2017.

Shepard, Wade, *Ghost Cities of China*, Zed Books, London, 2015.

Simpfendorfer, Ben, *The New Silk Road*, Palgrave Macmillan, London, 2009.

Smith, Hedrick, *Who Stole the American Dream?*, Random House, New York, 2012.

Steil, Benn, *The Battle of Bretton Woods*, Princeton University Press, Princeton, NJ, 2013.

Veronese, Keith, *Rare*, Prometheus Books, Buffalo, NY, 2015.

Walden, George, *China: A Wolf in the World?*, Gibson Square, London, 2008.

Wilkinson, Richard, and Pickett, Kate, *The Inner Level*, Allen Lane, London, 2018.

Wilkinson, Richard, and Pickett, Kate, *The Spirit Level*, Bloomsbury Press, London, 2009.

Index

About the Authors

Stephen Leeb, PhD, is a renowned expert on macro-perspectives of global economic trends. Leeb is the founder of Leeb Group, an investment management company based in New York, and editor of several subscription-based investment publications including the award-winning *The Complete Investor*. He is also the bestselling author of *The Oil Factor*, *The Coming Economic Collapse*, and *Game Over*.

Donna Leeb coauthored three of Stephen Leeb's previous books and is executive editor of *The Complete Investor*. She has a master's degree from Columbia University's Graduate School of Journalism.